Neolithic Archaeology in the Intertidal Zone

Neolithic Studies Group Seminar Papers 8

Edited by
Jane Sidell and Fiona Haughey

Oxbow Books

Published by
Oxbow Books, Oxford, UK

© Oxbow Books and the individual authors, 2007

ISBN 978 1 84217 266 7

This book is available direct from

Oxbow Books, Oxford, UK
(Phone: 01865-241249; Fax: 01865-794449)

and

The David Brown Book Company
PO Box 511, Oakville, CT06779
(Phone: 860-945-9329; Fax: 860-945-9468)

or

from our website
www.oxbowbooks.com

Cover: the Late Neolithic yew forest at Erith, South London.
Photo: Ellen Heppell

Printed in Great Britain by
The Information Press
Eynsham, Oxford

This book presents the proceedings of a seminar organised under the Neolithic Studies Group (NSG), forming part of an ongoing series of NSG seminar papers. The NSG is an informal organisation comprising archaeologists with an interest in Neolithic archaeology. It was established in 1984 and has a large membership based mainly in the UK and Ireland, but also including workers from the nations of the Atlantic seaboard. The annual programme includes two or three meetings spread throughout the year and includes seminars held in London and field meetings at various locations in north-west Europe.

Membership is open to anyone with an active interest in the Neolithic in Europe. The present membership includes academic staff and students, museums staff, archaeologists from government institutions, units, trusts and amateur organisations. There is no membership procedure or application forms and members are those on the current mailing list. Anyone can be added to the mailing list at any time, the only membership rule being that names of those who do not attend any of four consecutive meetings are removed from the list (in the absence of apologies for absence or requests to remain on the list).

The Group relies on the enthusiasm of its members to organise its annual meetings and the two co-ordinators to maintain mailing lists and finances. Financial support for the group is drawn from a small fee payable for attendance of each meeting.

Anyone wishing to contact the Group and obtain information about forthcoming meetings should contact the co-ordinators at the following addresses:

TIMOTHY DARVILL
School of Conservation Sciences
Bournemouth University
Poole
Dorset BH12 5BB

KENNETH BROPHY
Department of Archaeology
University of Glasgow
Glasgow
G12 8QQ

Alternatively visit the NSG website:

http://csweb.bournemouth.ac.uk/consci/text/nsghome.htm

Contents

Foreword by the Co-ordinators of the Neolithic Studies Group   iii
Preface   vii
List of Contributors   ix
List of Illustrations   xi

1   Small fragments of a bigger picture: coastal erosion and the Neolithic in the inner Solway Firth, southwest Scotland
Michael Cressey   1

2   Neolithic Coastal Archaeology and Environment around Liverpool Bay   11
Silvia Gonzalez and R. W. Cowell

3   Wetland-dryland relationships in the Severn Estuary and surroundings during the Mesolithic and Neolithic
Martin Bell   26

4   The Wootton Quarr Archaeological Survey, Isle of Wight   48
R. D. Loader

5   The Neolithic of the present day intertidal zone of Langstone Harbour, Hampshire
Michael J. Allen and Julie Gardiner   59

6   London, the backwater of Neolithic Britain? Archaeological Significance of Middle Holocene river and vegetation change in the London Thames   71
Keith Wilkinson and Jane Sidell

7   Searching for the Neolithic while it may be found: research in the inter-tidal zone of the London Thames   86
Fiona Haughey

8   Bibliography   95

This volume contains the bulk of papers presented at a one day meeting of the Neolithic Studies Group on Intertidal Archaeology in 1999. Sadly, this volume has been a long time in the making, owing to the usual pressures on archaeologists, some of whom were only able to submit after much time for cogitation, whilst others, unfortunately, were unable to submit their papers. The conference was held at a time when a growing awareness of the importance of intertidal archaeology was becoming widespread, and this has only increased over the intervening years, with much more fieldwork being undertaken in various estuaries such as the Humber and the Severn and on many coastal sites in the British Isles.

The intertidal zone is a remarkable one for archaeology – we find evidence for the very earliest occupants of the British Isles on the north Norfolk coast, literally on the beach at Happisburgh and Pakefield, and archaeology of every period since then may be found, right up to Second World War defences, now recorded archaeologically alongside more conventional archaeological structures. People have always been drawn to water for a variety of reasons, and of course water (plus mud and peat) preserves their remains well. Therefore, sites are found in higher concentrations in the intertidal zone, from everyday functional items, *i.e.* fish traps, through to the more elaborate, such as the timber circles at Holme-next-the-sea and of course human remains themselves.

However, over these last few years, along with an increased understanding of the prevalence and importance of these sites, we have also increased our knowledge of their fragility, but failed to devise ways of protecting them. Natural erosive processes are uncovering these sites for us, but they are also removing the sites after what can be an extremely short period of opportunity for study, sometimes as little as a half hour tide window. Simply put, such sites cannot easily be protected, either practically or by law. Many forms of preservation have been discussed, such as sandbagging, concreting and planting vegetation to try and retain sediment over these sites. Prevailing feeling within agencies tasked with coastal management and flood defence is that 'advancing the line', is simply not practical in the majority of areas of coastal erosion, and would only be considered if there was a high social and economic cost of not affording protection from the sea. Sadly, archaeology does not figure in this, and we must face up to the fact that much, if not all of our intertidal archaeology present in areas of active coastal erosion/ relative sea level rise, will be lost in time, and the likelihood is that as climate change continues, sites will be lost more rapidly. Therefore, it makes little sense to try and protect these sites by law, for instance by designating key sites as Scheduled Ancient Monuments. Nevertheless, the threat is real; it is estimated that the village of Happisburgh, where the cliffs contain some of the earliest evidence for hominin occupation of north-west Europe, may be lost to the sea within decades due to erosion of the cliff line.

This leaves us with the problem of how ensure these sites are recorded and understood before they are lost to us. This cannot be done via the planning process except in very exceptional cases where sites in the intertidal zone are developed, for instance where new jetties/pontoons are being inserted into the foreshore. In such cases, local authority curators can require that the sites in the area of impact are studied. This is, in itself not terribly satisfactory – it is unlikely that the whole of the 'site' will be contained within a limited footprint; however, this is a conundrum that terrestrial archaeologists have had to work with for some time. So it is rare that anyone can be paid via the commercial sector to record and analyse intertidal archaeology. Next we could look to our national heritage agencies to protect these sites. Sadly, as with the ecological agencies, national heritage agencies believe that sites at risk from natural erosion cannot all be funded; archaeological priorities have to be established at a national level, and to fund recording and research of all sites at risk from natural erosion would require significantly more than the available budget for archaeological research every year for the foreseeable future. Some money is available, and is being put into rapid coastal zone survey, but this only provides a baseline of the archaeology present; it does not move beyond basic quantification of the archaeological resource to recording and analysis of individual structures.

Next, can the universities help? It is clear in this volume that to an extent they can. However, it is a rare academic that is interested in intertidal archaeology, and whilst some areas, notably the Severn, are indeed being examined at the highest level, generally, very little effort is being put into the intertidal zone by British archaeological departments. Perhaps the logistical difficulties of the intertidal zone and problems of fund raising for research of the mudflats make this a rather low priority for 'academic' endeavour unlike more mainstream dryland sites.

So, where next? The voluntary sector. This covers a large body of people whose work has been and will continue to be invaluable. Intertidal sites need continual monitoring as well as sporadic fieldwork. Local societies are extremely well placed to undertake such monitoring, and working in liaison with other archaeologists can undertake suitable tranches of fieldwork which provide detailed and regular information on survival and state of preservation. Whilst this will not stop the sites from eroding, it will provide the vital record of the site. It also provides an opportunity for a greater range of people to participate in archaeological fieldwork; a rarer and rarer opportunity these days owing to the regulations surrounding commercial work, and the increasing costs of attending training digs.

Intertidal archaeology can be especially rewarding – sites covering a great range of periods and types, remarkable preservation and often with good regional coherence within estuaries or along coasts. However, such sites will not last for ever – thousands of years of occupation have been stripped away already, and it will not be long before many areas are stripped to bedrock. We have a responsibility to try to record what we can in this fantastic and dynamic zone before it is too late.

List of Contributors

MICHAEL J. ALLEN
Wessex Archaeology
Portway House
Old Sarum Park
Salisbury
Wiltshire SP4 6EB

MARTIN BELL
Department of Archaeology
University of Reading
Whiteknights
PO BOX 217
Reading RG6 6AH

R. W. COWELL
National Museums and Galleries
   on Merseyside
Liverpool Museum Field Archaeology
Unit, GWR Building, Mann Island
Liverpool L3 1DG

MICHAEL CRESSEY
CFA Archaeology Ltd
Suite 2
Archibald Hope House
Eskmills Park
East Lothian EH1 IJL

JULIE GARDINER
Wessex Archaeology
Portway House
Old Sarum Park
Salisbury
Wiltshire SP4 6EB

SILVIA GONZALEZ
School of Biological and Earth Sciences
Liverpool John Moores University
Byrom Street
Liverpool L3 3AF

FIONA HAUGHEY
Institute of Archaeology
31–34 Gordon Square
London WCIH OPY

REBECCA LOADER
Archaeological Centre
61 Clatterford Road
Carisbrooke
Isle of Wight
Newport
PO30 INZ

JANE SIDELL
Institute of Archaeology
31–34 Gordon Square
London WCIH OPY

KEITH WILKINSON
Department of Archaeology
King Alfred's University College
Winchester
SO22 4NB

FIGURES

1.1   General location.
1.2   Stratigraphic profiles of cliff sections at Sites A and B near Newbie Cottages.
1.3   Neolithic stone axe finds spots in eastern Dumfrieshire and the Solway Plain.
2.1   Localities in the NW of England with prehistoric evidence in the inter-tidal zone.
2.2   Stratigraphy and radiocarbon dates from some important inter-tidal zone localities around Liverpool Bay.
2.3   (a) Photograph of the original Victorian display recovered from the Preston Dock excavations. Reproduced by kind permission of the Harris Museum and Art Gallery, Preston. (b) Neolithic human skull 1997.70.7 showing hole in the back of the skull. Photo by S. Gonzalez.
2.4   (a) Location and distribution of the Formby Point Footprints (after Huddart *et al.* 1999a, b) and archaeological evidence south of the Altmouth (after Cowell and Innes 1994). (b) Composite stratigraphy of the sediments at Formby Point showing a change in environment for each of the two different sets of footprints (marked with black stars) (after Huddart *et. al.* 1999a).
2.5   Formby Point footprints examples: a) Human footprint. b) Aurochs footprint. Photos by S. Gonzalez.
2.6   Hightown Neolithic trackway. Photo by R. Cowell.
3.1   The Severn Estuary and Bristol Channel. (a) Location in Britain, arrow marks the Severn Estuary. (b) Coastline in *c.* 8200 Cal. BC and *c.* 6600 Cal BC (source Admiralty charts), in relation to the position of selected locations: Caldey; Gower; Goldcliff; Redwick; Westward Ho! (c) Distribution of Neolithic chambered tombs forming the Cotswold-Severn group (Source: Darvill 1982, fig. 2).
3.2   The distribution of Neolithic sites and findspots on dryland surrounding the Severn Estuary (for sources used see text).
3.3   The distribution of Neolithic findspots and pollen sequences in the Severn Estuary wetland (for details of pollen sites see Table 3.2).
3.4   Peterstone, Severn Estuary: (a) plan of palaeochannels of the Neolithic and Bronze Age (b) palaeochannel 3 with a wood stakes dated to the late Neolithic or early Bronze Age.
4.1   The location of sites mentioned in the text.
4.2   Neolithic post groups on Quarr Beach.
4.3   The sharpened points of two Neolithic posts. (Illustration by Ivor Westmore).
4.4   Neolithic trackways at low water at Quarr and Binstead.
4.5   Longshore trackway K27. Note the damaged rod that appears to have broken under the weight of a person or animal.
4.6   Flint axes recovered between Wootton Creek and Ryde.
4.7   Flint and chert axes recovered between Wootton Creek and Ryde.
4.8   Lithic scatters and axe findspots on the Wootton-Quarr coast.

4.9   Worked flint recovered from sites Q2 and Q99 on Quarr Beach.

4.10   Leaf arrowheads and microliths from sites Q2 and Q99 on Quarr Beach.

5.1   Location showing summary geology and location of Neolithic forest elements: BR = Baker's Rithe; RL = Russell's lake (drawn by S. E. James).

5.2   Model of stages of recession erosion showing artefact movement, redistribution across the intertidal zone, and ultimate loss in to the marine environment (drawn by S. E. James).

5.3   (a) Plan of the surviving Neolithic branches and tree stumps at Baker's Rithe peat shelf at *c.* -1m OD (drawn by S.E. James). b) Survey points of the main Neolithic branches and trunks at Russell's Lake peat shelf at *c.* -0.5m OD (data from Portsmouth University, drawn by S. E. James).

5.4   Reconstruction of the Langstone Harbour area in the Late Neolithic-Early Bronze Age (drawn by S. E. James).

6.1   Location of sites discussed in the text within London (Dorney, Eton Wick, and Yeoveney causewayed enclosure and the Mesolithic river channels at Staines are west of the main map).

6.2   Pollen diagram of Late Devensian glacial to late Holocene vegetation change in Silvertown (modified from Wilkinson *et al.*, 2000). Grey shading highlights the Neolithic period.

6.3   Sea level index points for Tilbury (mid estuary), Crossness (inner estuary) (Devoy, 1979), and central London after Long (1995) and Sidell *et al.* (2000). Grey shading highlights the Neolithic period.

6.4   Facies of the JLE plotted from west to east against a calibrated ^{14}C time scale (modified from Sidell *et al.*, 2000).

6.5   Pollen diagram of a Neolithic to Iron Age peat sequence at Union Street, Southwark (after Sidell *et al.*, 2000).

7.1   Location Map. 1 Bankside, 2 Barn Elms, 3 Battersea, 4 Bermondsey, 5 Blackfriars, 6 Chelsea, 7 Chiswick Eyot, 8 City of London, 9 Erith, 10 Greenwich, 11 Hammersmith, 12 Heathrow, 13 Mortlake, 14 Old England, 15 Putney, 16 Rainham, 17 Richmond, 18 Rotherhithe, 19 Syon Reach, 20 Teddington Lock, 21 Vauxhall, 22 Winchester Wharf.

7.2   Chelsea 'beater' (by permission of the Museum of London).

7.3   Peterborough Ware sherds from Bermondsey.

TABLES

1.1   Summary table of lithostratigraphic units, sediment type with Troels-Smith notation recorded in the cliffs at Newbie Cottages (Site A). The positions of the units are shown in Figure 1.2.

1.2   Summary of radiocarbon dates for the Newbie Cottages cliff section. All dates are calibrated using OxCal v 3.10.

2.1   AMS determinations and d13 values from remains from Preston Docks. Calibrated dates show 95% confidence range. After Turner *et al.* 2002.

3.1   The distribution of Neolithic sites and find spots on dry land surrounding the Severn estuary (for sources used, see text).

3.2   The distribution of Neolithic sites and find spots on dry land surrounding the Severn estuary (for sources used, see text).

5.1   Radiocarbon dates from submerged trees.

5.2   The tool assemblage excluding scrapers.

6.1   Correlation of chronological terminology and timescales (after Sidell *et al.*, 2000).

6.2   Beds, altitude and chronology of the Tilbury member (*sensu* Gibbard, 1994; Gibbard, 1999) after Devoy, (1979; 1980). Limits of Tilbury stages are defined by Thames event data.

Chapter 1

Small fragments of a bigger picture: coastal erosion and the Neolithic in the inner Solway Firth, southwest Scotland

Michael Cressey

ABSTRACT

The study area comprises a stretch of coastline, about 800m in length situated on the northern shore of the Inner Solway Firth between the coastal village of Powfoot and the mouth of the River Annan, Dumfries, south-west Scotland. This coastal zone is characterised by some of the fastest rates of cliff recession from within the Solway estuary. Further importance is attributed to this section of shoreline through its classification as a Geological Conservation Review Site (GCR site) that has a complete biostratigraphical record formed over the last 10,000 years. The cliffs have been the focus of very detailed palaeoenvironmental research culminating in the construction of a reliable record of sea level change. Bog-oaks have been exposed within the cliff section, and have been radiocarbon dated to the Mesolithic and Neolithic periods. The Neolithic assemblage has produced the second earliest dendrochronological non-structural timber in Scotland. The results from pollen and fossil wood analyses indicate that dense woodland prevailed during the Early Neolithic. Small inroads into the woodland are suggested which is in accord with more regional pollen diagrams from the area. The distribution of ground stone axes within the study area provides additional evidence for Neolithic activity.

INTRODUCTION

During the last 30 years a considerable amount of palaeoenvironmental research, principally concerned with former patterns of sea level change, has been undertaken in the Solway lowlands (Jardine 1971; 1975; 1980a and b). Jardine's programme of work along the northern shoreline of the Solway Firth involved geomorphological mapping, stratigraphical investigations and radiocarbon dating. More recent studies have built on his investigations examining old and newly discovered sites to develop a more detailed picture of relative sea level changes in the area (Wells 1999). The combined use of diatom, pollen, foraminifers, ostracods and molluscs in conjunction with single-entity AMS radiocarbon dating and more recently, dendrochronology has led to a revision on the timing of relative sea level change in the Inner Solway Firth (cf. Cressey *et al.* 1998; Milburn and Tipping 1999; Haggart 1999; Dawson *et al.* 1999 and Wells 1999). Changes in relative sea level have serious implications for palaeoshoreline modelling, site formation dynamics, and importantly for archaeology in the prehistoric period.

Continuous coastal erosion has taken its toll on cultural heritage within the Inner Solway Firth. At Redkirk Point (NGR:NY320651) 2km west of Gretna Green, the presence of a Mesolithic hearth and flint scatter is recorded (Masters 1981) along with the vestigial remains of a dug-out boat (NMRS). The placename Redkirk Point is derived from a 14th century church (*Red Kirk*) with graveyard, which is reputed to have been lost due to coastal erosion. Scatters of medieval pottery, possibly associated with that site are also recorded. In 1856 two Bronze Age cist burials and remnants of an 'ancient forest' were found exposed within the eroding cliff section near Newbie Mains (NGR:NY171646) (Jardine 1863–64).

Based partly on the findings of a rapid coastal assessment of the entire Scottish side of the Solway Firth (Cressey and Toolis 1996), Historic Scotland commissioned further work on eroding shorelines close to the town of Annan, East Dumfriesshire (Figure 1.1). A collaborative project was carried out by the Universities of Stirling, Coventry and Edinburgh (Cressey *et al.* 1998 and Cressey *et al.* 2001) using a range of palaeoenvironmental techniques to establish the nature and quality of information preserved within the deposits. As an adjunct to this work, a further phase of research was undertaken during 1999 to recover sub-fossil wood from eroding cliffs at Broom Knowes to the west of Newbie Cottages. An evaluation on behalf of Scottish Natural Heritage (SNH), was also undertaken to explore the options for the future conservation management of a section of the Newbie Cottages shoreline classified as a Geological Conservation Review site (Cressey 2001). The site is also part of a much larger Site of Special Scientific Interest, namely the Upper Solway Flats and Marshes.

The results of biostratigraphic recording on two sections of the Newbie cliff sections where fossil wood is exposed are summarised here. Their significance in terms of Neolithic woodland composition is assessed in relation to other proxy strands of evidence further inland drawing primarily on the results of pollen analyses and more indirectly on the regional distribution of Neolithic axes.

BIOSTRATIGRAPHIC PROFILES AT NEWBIE COTTAGES

Two main sections in the study area are considered here. The first site is a cliff section at Newbie Cottages (Site A); the second (Site B) is situated *c.* 200m further west (Figures 1.1 and 1.2). Both sites share the same stratigraphy, although the dune sand and palaeosol sequence at Site B is disturbed by rabbit infestation and was not recorded in detail. At Site A, samples were obtained from the organic horizons (Units 1, 2, 4, 6, 10, 12, and 14) using Kubiena tins. Contiguous pollen and diatom samples were extracted from these bulk samples. Radiocarbon samples were obtained from critical contact zones.

The Neolithic period is represented by an extensive deposit of peat (Site A, Unit 6 in Figure 1.2), which continues westwards for almost 500m. In order to place this horizon in its stratigraphic context a full description of the profile is described (Table 1.1).

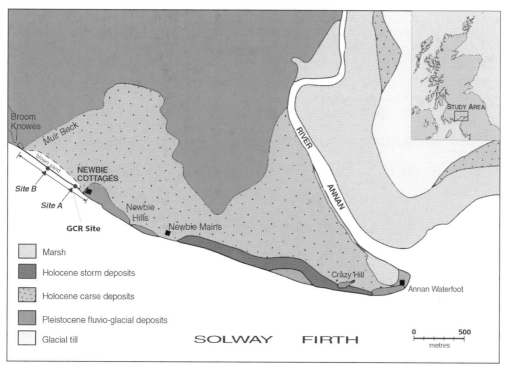

Figure 1.1 General location

Units in Figure 1.2	Description	Troels-Smith (1955) notation
16	root mat	
15	sand	Ga4
14	humic palaeosol C	Sh3 Ga1 Dh+ Th+
13	sand	Ga4
12	humic palaeosol B	Sh3 Ga1 Dh+ Th+
11	sand	Ga4
10	humic palaeosol A	Sh3 Ga1 Dh+ Th+
9	sand	Ga4
8	peat	Sh4 Dh+ Th+
7	sand	Ga4
6	peat	Sh4 Ga+Dh+ Th+
5	grey carse clay	As4 D1 Dh+ Th+
4	carse peat	As4 Sh+Dh+TH+
3	grey carse clay	As4 D1 Dh+ Th+
2	intertidal woody peat	Sh4 D1+ Dh+ Th+
1	boulder clay/sand/gravel	As1 Ag1 Ga1 Gs1 Gg (min)+ Gg (maj)+

Table 1.1 Summary table of lithostratigraphic units, sediment type with Troels-Smith notation recorded in the cliffs at Newbie Cottages (Site A). The positions of the units are shown in Figure 1.2.

Michael Cressey

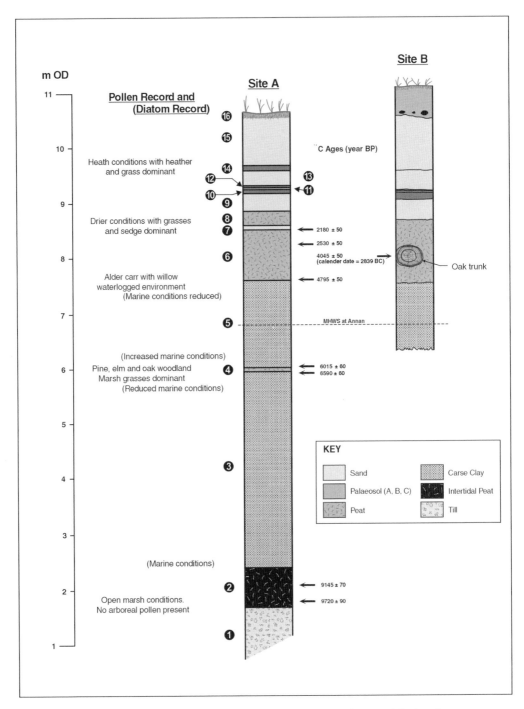

Figure 1.2 Stratigraphic profiles of cliff sections at Sites A and B near Newbie Cottages

Newbie Cottages Lithostratigraphy and Environment

The lithostratigraphy exposed in the cliff was earlier described by Jardine (1975), but until the more recent investigations, the intertidal peat remained unrecorded. This layer (Unit 2) is visible about 20m south of the base of the cliff where sub-fossil tree stumps and the eroded surface of the peat are well exposed at low tide. Towards the base of the cliff, the peat is masked by recent beach deposits and up to 5m of carse clay (Units 3 and 5). The carse clay at and above the 2.5m OD position is very compact and remains uniform until at 6m OD where an organic peat layer is present (Unit 4). Carse clay continues above this layer until the 7.5m OD position where a well-humified woody peat (Unit 6) commences until 8.6m OD. The basal and upper contact boundaries of this unit are sharp. Beyond this layer, dune sand is inter-banded with three palaeosol horizons (Units 10, 12 and 14) that vary in thickness.

Radiocarbon dating results

Nine samples were submitted to the Scottish Universities Research and Reactor Centre and AMS dates were obtained from the humic acid fraction on 5mm sections of sediment recovered from specific contact zones in this stratigraphical sequence (see Table 1.2 overleaf). In the case of the oak stump recovered from the middle of Unit 6 at Site B, the sample for AMS dating was obtained on the bark and cambium layer interface, the latter representing the outermost tree-ring.

Results from dendrochronological dating from Site B

Four oak stumps were recorded adjacent to Site B. From samples obtained from each of these, individual sequences were compared with a series of master chronologies from England and Ireland. Only the largest tree stump (NC1) at Site B produced significant correlation with master chronologies from England and Ireland respectively dating the 264 tree-ring sequence to 3112–2849 cal BC (Crone 1998). The addition of a minimum of 10 rings to account for the missing sapwood (Hillam *et al.* 1987) provides a *terminus post quem* of 2839 cal BC. NC1 therefore stopped growing early in the first half of the 3rd millennium cal BC. This determination is currently the earliest dendrochronologically dated (supported by radiocarbon dating) non-structural oak in Scotland (Crone 1998).

LOCAL SEDIMENT-FORMING SITE DYNAMICS BASED ON POLLEN AND DIATOM ANALYSES

The results of pollen and diatom analyses are summarised below and in Figure 1.2. A more detailed account of this research is given in Dawson *et al.* 1999 and Cressey *et al.* (2001).

Palaeoenvironmental reconstruction

The pollen and radiocarbon dating evidence both correlate well with continuous palaeoecological records from nearby peat deposits (Lloyd 1999; Wells 1999). Treeless

Michael Cressey

Site	Lab code	Position	Height (OD)	Radiocarbon measurement	Calibrated date BC (95% confidence)	Calibrated date BP (95% confidence)
Newbie Cottages	AA-30341	Base Unit 2	1.5m	9720 ± 90	9350-8800 cal BC	7400-6850 cal BP
Newbie Cottages	AA-30342	Middle Unit 2	2.5m	9145 ± 70	8550-8250 cal BC	6600-6300 cal BP
Newbie Cottages	AA-30343	Base Unit 4	6.0m	6590 ± 65	5640-5380 cal BC	3690-3430 cal BP
Newbie Cottages	AA-30344	Top Unit 4	6.1m	6015 ± 60	5060-4720 cal BC	3110-2770 cal BP
Newbie Cottages	AA-30346	Base Unit 6	7.6m	4795 ± 50	3660-3370 cal BC	1710-1420 cal BP
NC1-4 Fossil Oak	AA-30345	NC1 Oak	7.9m	4045 ± 50	2860-2460 cal BC	910-510 cal BP
Newbie Cottages	AA-30347	Middle Unit 6	8.0m	2530 ± 50	810-410 cal BC	1140-740 cal BP
Newbie Cottages	AA-30348	Top Unit 6	8.5m	2180 ± 50	390-100 cal BC	1560-1850 cal BP

Table 1.2 Summary of radiocarbon dates for the Newbie Cottages cliff section. All dates are calibrated using OxCal v 3.10

environments persisted into the early Holocene in the coastal area around the Solway, and the development of extensive woodland occurred locally after *c.*7000 cal BC. By 4500 cal BC mixed deciduous woodland was established and was still present shortly after the elm decline (*c.* 4800 BP). This record in itself gives no insight either into the timing or causes of woodland decline, but anthropogenic influences are considered to be important towards the upland areas in SW Scotland (Tipping 1999). By 2200 BP the landscape was predominantly open, although some surviving woodland fragments are inferred. The results obtained from the Newbie Cottages section Units 1, 4 and 6 (Figure 1.2) are summarised on hereafter.

The intertidal peat. Unit 2 (9700–9150 BP) Mesolithic
Pollen analysis of the basal sediments from this unit indicates that it was deposited in a fresh-water, sedge-dominated marsh community. Diatom analysis from the boundary between this unit and the overlying carse intimate that these sediments were deposited in a lower intertidal environment with increasing marine influence across the transition. This suggests marine encroachment onto a freshwater marsh in the Early Holocene.

The carse peat. Unit 4 (6600–6000 BP) Late Mesolithic–Early Neolithic
Diatom analysis across the lower boundary of this unit suggests that this transition represents a regressive sea-level index point, with a reduction in salinity and marine influence as the peat developed. Pollen analysis from the centre of this unit implies it was deposited under open, marshy vegetation, with a fluctuating water table. Diatom analysis from the upper edge of the peat suggests deposition just above MHWST. Samples from the overlying carse show increasing marine influence with renewed marine transgression.

The overlying peat. Unit 6 (4800–2200 BP) Neolithic-Iron Age
Diatom analysis across the transition shows a reduction in marine influence as the peat unit is approached, demonstrating that the boundary is a regressive sea-level index point. The pollen assemblage from the base of the peat suggests alder carr was locally present, which implies low to non-existent marine influence. A mixed oak-birch woodland co-existed alongside an alder carr environment. The pollen results are corroborated by the sub-fossil remains of oak and birch stumps, which are locally exposed towards the base of Unit 6 at Site B.

Pollen analysis suggests that the upper boundary of the unit, dated to 2200 BP, was deposited under a more open vegetation community, dominated by grasses but possibly with some heaths. More detailed study would be needed to investigate the cause of this change.

Above Unit 6, a series of organic palaeosols (Units 10, 12 and 14) interspersed with sands suggest an active coastal environment and a complex history of dune evolution in the last two millennia. Pollen assemblages from single samples within the palaeosols show that these horizons developed in an open environment of heathland that was possibly grazed.

DISCUSSION OF THE WIDER IMPLICATIONS

The palaeoenvironmental information obtained from Unit 6 within the Newbie Cottage profile (Site A), allows an accurate reconstruction on the timing of the culmination of the Holocene Marine Transgression which ceased at 4795 ± 50 BP (3600–3370 cal BC) (see Figure 1.2). A skeleton pollen diagram was constructed for Newbie Cottages (Cressey *et al.* 2001) and links with other regional pollen diagrams have been successfully established. On the basis of these results we can envisage that during the early part of the Neolithic, the landscape close to the main channel of the River Esk was wooded with stands of oak and birch. Alder and willow thrived close to freshwater streams. During the Middle Neolithic (*c.* 2500 cal BC), dense oak forest fringed with stands of birch became established in areas less prone to waterlogging. Oak and birch exposed in the cliff section at Site B were recovered as recumbent trunks with no evidence to suggest they had been felled. Others were still in an upright position, as they would have grown. This seems to suggest the trees died of natural causes perhaps due to the emergence of blanket peat which continued to develop as a result of wetter conditions augmented by fluctuations in climate, and perhaps more importantly, increased surface run-off from the surrounding catchment. It is not until the Early Bronze Age that the local soils were rendered suitable for agriculture as is evidenced by the presence of palaeosols, which are laterally extensive between Site A, and Site B.

Tipping (1997) notes that the first clearings for agriculture can be detected in the lowlands from the beginning of the 4th millennium cal BC, but similar evidence (*e.g.* increases in micro-charcoal, the presence of cereal pollen and open ground taxa) is not as frequent in the palynological record. He also suggests that farmers did not move into the uplands in any numbers at this early date despite the presence of probable Neolithic monuments in the upland region (cf. figure 86 RCAHMS 1997).

The archaeological record for the Neolithic period on the Scottish side of the Inner Solway Firth is fragmentary and until new sites are identified within the study area we have to use other evidence based on lithic distribution and vegetation changes in the palynological record. Barclay (1997) has noted that aerial photography during the last 20 years reveals a dense hitherto unsuspected distribution of Neolithic and Early Bronze Age timber and turf monuments, most now ploughed out but some nevertheless well preserved in lowland east and south-west Scotland. It is argued that cropmark evidence for this period within the Inner Solway Firth may be of little use in locating sites owing to the predominance of peat and carse clays that may have effectively masked them. On soils other than peat and carse clays, negative features such as pits and post holes may not be detectable as crop marks owing to pastoral land use. Neolithic settlement evidence has tended to be found as a product of ground disturbance, as in pipeline construction. The site of Blairhall Burn, Amisfield, near Dumfries (Strachan *et al.* 1998) is a good example. It was here, during the construction of a pipeline that two Neolithic pits containing pottery and a fragment of a Group VI axe were recovered. Charcoal from one of these pits produced a radiocarbon date of 3500–3440 cal BC (Beta 73951). Strachan notes that without further excavation it is not clear if these features are isolated remains or part of a larger Neolithic complex centred outside the excavated area. Ashmore (1996) has considered more extensive settlement evidence in a wider context with other ritual monuments in the lower Annan valley. Within Eastern Dumfriesshire the distribution of

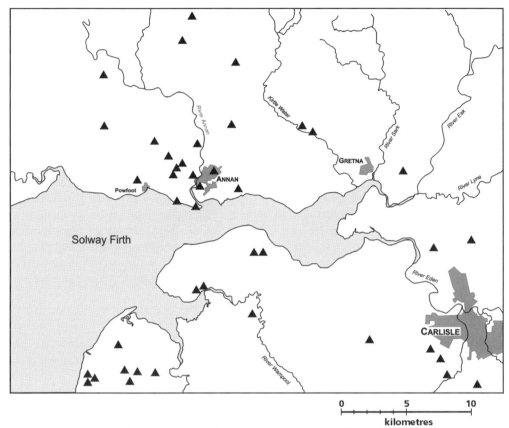

Figure 1.3 Neolithic stone axe finds spots in eastern Dumfrieshire and the Solway Plain

henge monuments and stone circles combined with that of stone axes shows that the landscape was extensively exploited in the Neolithic, although the palynological evidence supports the theory that little of this activity had a serious impact on the lowland woodland landscape. Cursus monuments and bank barrows show a pronounced cluster on the fluvioglacial terraces on either side of the River Nith north of Dumfries. These monuments in association with other features such as standing stones and stone circles have been mapped by RCAHMS (cf. figure 86, *Eastern Dumfriesshire* RACHMS 1997).

Finds of Neolithic Group VI stone axes are fairly common in East Dumfriesshire (Figure 1.3) with a noticeable cluster occurring to the west of Annan. Similar finds are also widely distributed in the Solway Plain in England (Bewley 1994, figures 4.1 and 4.2). This series of axes comprise epidotized intermediate tuff of the Borrowdale Volcanic series from the Great Langdale and Scafell areas of Cumbria (Williams 1970 and Bewley 1994). Tipping (1999 *infra*) rightly mentions that the axe distribution could be biased because of recent population density, antiquarian interests and chance finds following ploughing. The apparent cluster of axes near Annan is intriguing but perhaps not unexpected given the close proximity to the parent source.

CONCLUSION

The results of this research have implications for understanding when successive vegetation changes occurred following the regression of the sea to its current position at around 3500 cal BC. The dendrochronology results on the oak stump from Site B have provided the second earliest dated non-structural wood in Scotland. The fact that climax oak forest was not only well established, but was probably extremely dense along the coastal fringes in the Annan area is of great significance. With the inception of blanket peat, and subsequent spread of alder carr, the landscape near the coast would not have been suitable for cultivation. However, small inroads into the later Neolithic woodland were made according to the local pollen stratigraphy and this is in accord with the regional pollen record established by Tipping *et al.* 1999 and co-workers. The distribution of stone tools in the Inner Solway Firth, including the Solway Plain provide indirect evidence for Neolithic activity suggesting small scale woodland clearance. The recent shoreline investigations at Newbie Cottages are supported by seven AMS radiocarbon dates that allow greater chronological precision than the conventional radiocarbon dates previously obtained from bulk samples (Jardine 1975). The AMS dates combined with biostratigraphical analyses provide a better understanding on the timing of relative sea level change and local site formation dynamics during the Neolithic Period.

ACKNOWLEDGEMENTS

This research would not have been possible without the financial support from Historic Scotland, Scottish Natural Heritage and the Society of Antiquaries for Scotland. The author wishes to thank Professor Alaistair Dawson and Drs Susan Dawson, Jane Bunting, Paula Milburn, Debora Long and Anne Crone for their input in both the field and laboratory during *Solway Phase 2*. The landowner Mr Goldie of Newbie Mains Farm is thanked for access to the site and technical support during the fieldwork. George Mudie and Kevin Hicks are thanked for their assistance with illustrations.

Chapter 2

Neolithic Coastal Archaeology and Environment around Liverpool Bay

Silvia Gonzalez and R. W. Cowell

INTRODUCTION

Recent work in the intertidal areas and flanking wetlands of the NW of England around Liverpool Bay has seen a big advance in our understanding of the nature of prehistoric settlement and environment in the area. The coast and river estuaries are now seen as key areas for answering many questions about the development of human use of the prehistoric landscape.

Several important archaeological sites in the intertidal zone around Liverpool Bay have been studied recently including Preston Docks, on the River Ribble and Formby Point and Hightown, both in Merseyside (Figure 2.1). The archaeological and palaeoenvironmental evidence obtained so far is reviewed in this paper with the focus on the Neolithic period. The deposits in which the archaeological evidence has been found in general consist of sequences of Late Pleistocene till deposits at the base, on top of which are found several Holocene layers of blue silt/clay, associated with marine transgressions and interbedded with peat horizons. All the sequences finish with the deposition of sand dunes. The general stratigraphy at each location mentioned in this paper together with radiocarbon dates is shown in Figure 2.2.

The stratigraphy shows that during the last 9000 years the low-lying coastal areas of NW England and North Wales experienced a total sea level rise of 20m (Tooley 1978), due to the melting of ice caps from the last glacial period producing rapid changes in the coastal/ river mouth environments. Sea level changes have meant that many of the non-marine sediments formed during the latter part of the Holocene are now buried at or about the intertidal zone of the present day shoreline, and can be seen from time to time uncovered in coastal lowland or estuarine localities. Interbedded peats, silts and sands occur at various points along this shoreline and in the estuarine deposits of the rivers of the region (Figure 2.2), often preserving considerable quantities of biotic material in the form of tree stumps, diatoms, foraminifera, ostracods and vertebrate remains (including human), as well as archaeological artefacts. This evidence provides the basis for identifying the environmental changes experienced in the coastal areas during the last 9000 years BP. These changes have been an important control on the nature and development of prehistoric human activity in the coastal lowlands (Cowell and Innes 1994; Roberts *et al.* 1996; Gonzalez *et al.* 1997; Huddart *et al.* 1999 a,b).

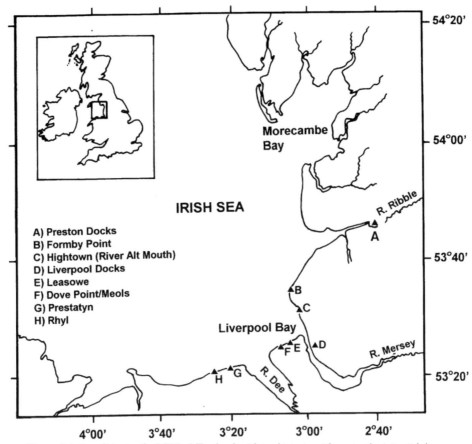

Figure 2.1 Localities in the NW of England with prehistoric evidence in the inter-tidal zone

The detailed stratigraphic, palaeoenvironmental and archaeological evidence at three locations along the coast of what was formerly south Lancashire, at Preston Docks, Formby Point and Hightown is reviewed in the following sections. An attempt is then made to set the evidence from the Merseyside part of this coastline into a model of land-use and settlement in the Neolithic period.

PRESTON DOCK COLLECTION

Investigation of institutional collections of animal and human collections recovered from Holocene deposits around Liverpool Bay brought to our attention the Preston Docks bone collection, held in the Harris Museum and Art Gallery in Preston. During the excavation works for the Preston Docks during the 1880's a large sample of human and other animal crania were recovered from the estuarine deposits of the River Ribble at Preston in Lancashire. The material has long been recognised as being of intrinsic archaeological

NW England Intertidal Zone Sites

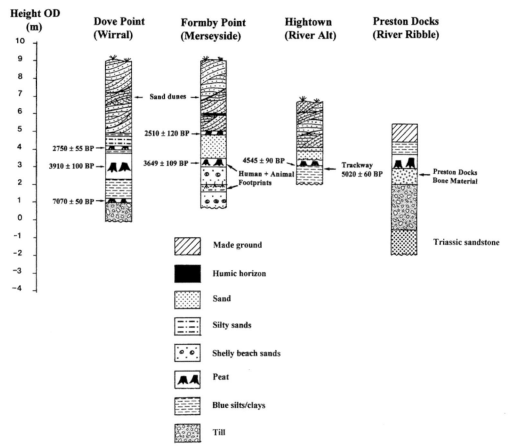

Figure 2.2 Stratigraphy and radiocarbon dates from some important inter-tidal zone localities around Liverpool Bay.

interest, since the presence of aurochs (*Bos primigenius*) in the collection suggested a probable Bronze Age date at least for the finds.

The material described originally by Dickson (1888), included 20 human crania, 60 pairs of red deer antlers (*Cervus elaphus*), 43 aurochs skulls, two pilot whales (*Sphaerocephalus incrassatus*) and a portion of the left jaw of the razor back whale (*Physalus antiquorum*) plus a few postcrania of horse (*Equus ferus*). A few artefacts, including two dugout boats, a bronze spearhead and a brushwood platform 17m by 17m in extent (Cole 1890), were reported from the general vicinity, but the bones have no archaeological context. Remains of the two boats are available in the Harris Museum, one complete and on display (1997.71.2), the other in fragments (1997.71.1). The animal remains and boats formed an impressive display at the Harris Museum at the beginning of the 20th century (Figure 2.3a).

The excavations took place in the Ribble alluvial plain, where the stratigraphic sequence

Laboratory Number	Specimen Number	Species	δ¹³C	AMS BP	Calibrated date
OxA-7410	1997.53.2	*Cervus elaphus*	-22.3	2730±40	980–800 cal BC
OxA-7411	1997.53.6	*Cervus elaphus*	-22.3	2865±45	1200–900 cal BC
OxA-7505	1997.53.13	*Cervus elaphus*	-22.3	3860±80	2570–2040 cal BC
OxA-7412	1997.54.1	*Bos primigenius*	-22.0	3495±40	1930–1690 cal BC
OxA-7413	1997.54.2	*Bos primigenius*	-22.3	4320±45	3090–2870 cal BC
OxA-7414	1997.54.3	*Bos primigenius*	-22.8	4235±45	2920–2660 cal BC
OxA-9291	1997.70.1	*Homo sapiens*	-19.9	1980±40	90 cal BC–130 cal AD
OxA-71415	1997.70.4	*Homo sapiens*	-21.13	4625±45	3630–3130 cal BC
OxA-71416	1997.70.7	*Homo sapiens*	-21.3	4370±45	3270–2890 cal BC
OxA-71417	1997.70.11	*Homo sapiens*	-21.5	4640±45	3630–3340 cal BC
OxA-71418	1997.70.13	*Homo sapiens*	-21.1	3380±40	1770–1530 cal BC
OxA-71419	1997.70.14	*Homo sapiens*	-21.0	4835±55	3720–3380 cal BC
OxA-9292	1997.70.17	*Homo sapiens*	-19.6	1244±30	680–870 cal AD
OxA-71420	1997.70.19	*Homo sapiens*	-21.1	4965±55	3840–3640 cal BC

Table 2.1 AMS determinations and δ13 values from remains from Preston Docks. Calibrated dates show 95% confidence range. After Turner et al. 2002.

was: surface soil, river silt, brown mottled sand, peat, sand and coarse gravel overlying Triassic sandstone (Dickson 1887, and Figure 2.2). The bones from the aurochsen and red deer were found together in the sand and coarse gravel, usually 3.5 to 5m below the surface, at 1.5 to 2m above OD. Although it is thought that the human crania came from the gravel, De Rance (1888) thought that they came from the overlying alluvial sediments along with the other mammalian remains. It was not known why such a large number of bones was deposited in this location, but examination of the human crania indicate that some show some signs of violence, such as cut marks and holes, particularly on the back of the skull, suggesting a violent death. This suggests the possibility of ceremonial/sacrificial killing.

With this background, a detailed programme of study of the bone collection was undertaken to describe, measure and radiocarbon date some of the specimens to try to understand the overall bone assemblage. The results are reported in Turner *et al.* 2002. A preliminary examination of the material located a total of 23 human crania, 21 aurochs crania or fragments of crania, 25 fragmentary red deer crania with antlers plus several isolated antlers and a broken cranium and a small number of aurochs, red deer and horse postcrania plus some cetacean remains. It showed that the human and animal bone were in excellent preservation state and suitable for radiocarbon dating. The results of the dating programme are summarised in Table 2.1. The method used to date the Preston Dock collection was Accelerator Mass Spectrometry (AMS) due to the fact that only a very small sample was required, less than 2gm. The dates were obtained at the Oxford Radiocarbon Accelerator Unit with a grant from the ORADS programme from NERC. Dates have been calibrated using OxCal v 3.10 (Bronk Ramsey 2001) using the calibration curve of Reimer *et al.* (2004) and quoted after Mook 1986.

In total, fourteen crania were selected for dating; three red deer, three aurochs, eight human and the two boats. The bone specimens gave good reliable results but the boats

Figure 2.3 (a) Photograph of the original Victorian display recovered from the Preston Dock excavations. Reproduced by kind permission of the Harris Museum and Art Gallery, Preston. (b) Neolithic human skull 1997.70.7 showing hole in the back of the skull. Photo by S. Gonzalez.

were too contaminated to give reliable dates (Pettitt and Hodgins *in litt.*). The span of the dates is considerable, around 4500 years. All the studied specimens have $\delta^{13}C$ values indicative of entirely terrestrial diets (Richards and Hedges 1999). These results are surprising considering that the human bone material was found close to the estuary of the River Ribble.

Five of the eight human crania are Neolithic in age with dates falling in the fourth millennium cal BC on calibrated ages, one (1997.70.13) is Bronze Age, one (1997.70.1) is Romano British and one (1997.70.17) is of Saxon age. Two of the aurochsen are Neolithic, closer to the earlier human group; the other aurochs together with the three red deer are later than 1000 cal BC.

The fact that most of the Preston human crania do not show excessive evidence of transportation damage, despite being found in gravels, might be used to argue for deliberate placement in the River Ribble, having first been removed from the body and separated from the mandibles. However, we know from the AMS dating that the human and animal remains were not deposited in a single event involving death of all at the same time.

Six human specimens (numbers 1997.70.1, 7, 11, 13, 14 and 17) appear to bear some evidence of trauma, including perforations (1, 7, 11), a depression fracture (8) and cut-marks (11, 13, 14, and 17). Three of these specimens are Neolithic in age (7, 11 and 14). Figure 2.3b shows a female Neolithic skull 1997.70.7 with a large hole in the back of the skull, with a date of 3270–2890 cal BC.

Isolated and usually undated human crania from riverine deposits in the British Isles present something of an archaeological mystery (Bradley and Gordon 1988; Bradley, 1995; Knüsel and Carr 1995; 1996). The numbers involved (several hundred from the River Thames alone) together with the recovery of unassociated metal artefacts have been taken to imply "ritual" activity. However, a series of AMS determinations on human crania, aurochsen (*Bos primigenius*) and red deer (*Cervus elaphus*) from the Preston Dock collection has established at least a Neolithic to Saxon age range age for the specimens. This chronological span for such a diverse assemblage, when considered against modern forensic

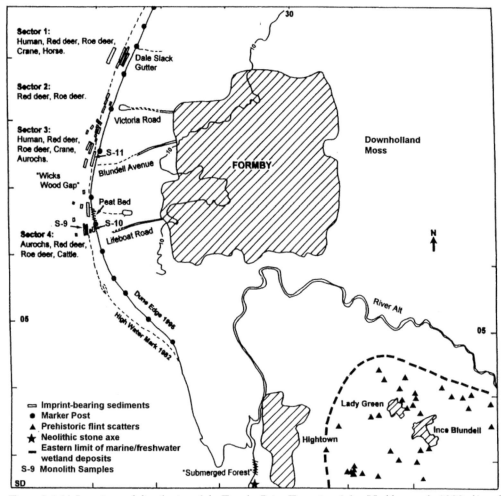

Figure 2.4 (a) Location and distribution of the Formby Point Footprints (after Huddart et al. *1999a,b) and archaeological evidence south of the Altmouth (after Cowell and Innes 1994).*

studies of the taphonomy of bodies in water, strongly supports the presence of human and animal skulls in the riverbed gravels as the result of an accumulation of elements that normally separate naturally from the rest of the body. While the reasons for initial entry to the river may well have included "ritual activity" in one or more cases, there is so far no reason to infer such behaviour for all the human and animal material from the Preston Dock collection.

Further to the south, in Merseyside, two sites of this period, at Formby Point and at Hightown in the District of Sefton (Figure 2.1) have been recorded recently in the inter-tidal zone. These are augmented by a body of evidence from fieldwalking inland of the coastal fringe, mainly as a result of the English Heritage sponsored North West Wetland

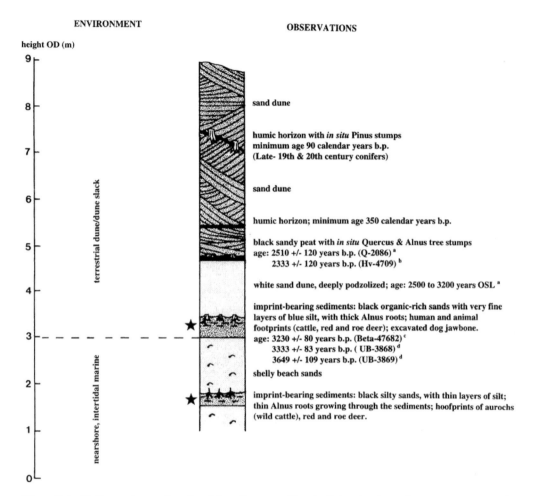

ENVIRONMENT   OBSERVATIONS

height OD (m)

sand dune

humic horizon with *in situ* Pinus stumps
minimum age 90 calendar years b.p.
(Late- 19th & 20th century conifers)

sand dune

humic horizon; minimum age 350 calendar years b.p.

black sandy peat with *in situ* Quercus & Alnus tree stumps
age: 2510 +/- 120 years b.p. (Q-2086)[a]
      2333 +/- 120 years b.p. (Hv-4709)[b]

white sand dune, deeply podzolized; age: 2500 to 3200 years OSL[a]

imprint-bearing sediments: black organic-rich sands with very fine
layers of blue silt, with thick Alnus roots; human and animal
footprints (cattle, red and roe deer); excavated dog jawbone.
age: 3230 +/- 80 years b.p. (Beta-47682)[c]
      3333 +/- 83 years b.p. (UB-3868)[d]
      3649 +/- 109 years b.p. (UB-3869)[d]

shelly beach sands

imprint-bearing sediments: black silty sands, with thin layers of silt;
thin Alnus roots growing through the sediments; hoofprints of aurochs
(wild cattle), red and roe deer.

terrestrial dune/dune slack

nearshore, intertidal marine

Figure 2.4 (b) Composite stratigraphy of the sediments at Formby Point showing a change in environment for each of the two different sets of footprints (marked with black stars) (after Huddart et al. 1999a)

Survey (Cowell and Innes 1994), although the discussion here only takes account of the results from south of the River Alt, in Merseyside (Figure 2.4a). The publication deadline for this paper has not allowed consideration of the data from the area to the north, in West Lancashire, which is in the process of being published (Middleton *et al.* in press). The Sefton work can be set in the wider context of field survey away from the coastal wetland fringe (Cowell 1991a; 2000a; 2000b). There are also a number of important pollen sites which have been investigated in the area, following the work of Michael Tooley and Jim Innes, which provide a vegetational framework to aid the interpretations of human activity in this coastal belt (Cowell and Innes 1994; Middleton *et al.* in press).

Figure 2.5 Formby Point footprints examples: a) Human footprint. b) Aurochs footprint. Photos by S. Gonzalez

FORMBY POINT FOOTPRINTS

Formby Point is part of the Sefton Coast dune system, which occupies 1285 hectares, forming a natural coastal defence some 15km long and 4km wide at its maximum extent and locally rising to 30m above sea level. This coastal dune barrier has been influenced by processes both in the Ribble and Mersey estuaries and in the eastern Irish Sea (Pye 1990).

Strong tidal currents and moderate wave energy conditions of the eastern Irish Sea dominate present day sediment transport and deposition. The result is a predominantly sandy, multi-barred foreshore (Parker 1975) backed by coastal dunes, which are of major conservation importance in a European context for animals and plants (Atkinson and Houston 1993).

The coastal sediments in this locality preserve a record of changing geomorphology and sea level rise for much of the Holocene and they provide evidence for the changing palaeoenvironments along this coastline in contrast to the extensive areas of peat mossland inland from the dune barrier. The nature of the marine transgressions, their recognition and understanding are crucial to the understanding of the prehistoric archaeology (Cowell and Innes 1994).

Figure 2.6 Hightown Neolithic trackway. Photo by R. Cowell

Large numbers of prehistoric human and animal footprints (aurochs, red deer, roe deer, dog) and animal bones (aurochs, red deer jawbone and complete unshed antlers, dog jawbone) preserved in the beach sediments at Formby Point, Merseyside have been reported during the last 30 years (Tooley 1970; Cowell *et al.* 1993; Pye and Neal 1994; Roberts *et al.* 1996; Gonzalez *et al.* 1997; Huddart *et al.* 1999a; 1999b). Gordon Roberts began systematically recording the animal and bird footprints in 1989 and the human footprints in 1990 and a selective photographic archive of over 3000 photos has been made, including details of 145 human footprint trails. They appear discontinuously in a 4km belt within the Holocene sediments (centred on GR SD 2606), within a 100m wide belt in the intertidal zone, usually about 60m west of the dune edge (Figure 2.4a). Some footprint examples are shown in Figure 2.5. The exposure of these sediments is due to the rapid erosion of the beach and dunes at Formby Point, where the sand dunes have an average rate of erosion of up to 3m per year (Pye and Neal 1994).

Recent work suggests that the animal and human footprints are at least as old as 3350–1730 cal BC. However, there are two stratigraphic sets of footprints and it is the younger that it is of this age (Gonzalez *et al.* 1997; Roberts *et al.* 1996). The sediments in which the older prints were made have been shown to be nearshore, intertidal marine sediments, based on the sedimentology and micro- and macrofossil evidence. The younger prints are associated with the lowest sedimentary units in a dune/dune slack environment (Figure 2.4b)

HIGHTOWN TRACKWAY

About 4km to the south, on the present beach at Hightown, where the river Alt flows into the Irish Sea north of the mouth of the Mersey (Figure 2.4a), a 2m length of a timber brushwood feature, just under 0.30m in depth and 1.4m wide, was recently excavated (Cowell *et al.* in prep). It was made up of longitudinal roundwood with oblique members woven in at the lower level (Figure 2.6), with a more haphazard arrangement of timbers at the upper level. Radiocarbon determinations have been obtained for the structure of 3960–3690 cal BC (Beta-119008, 5020±60 BP) and 3920–3520 cal BC (Beta-119010, 4910±60

BP). A roundwood with facetted point, driven vertically into the underlying clay to a depth of *c.* 1m, produced a radiocarbon date of 3350–2910 cal BC (Beta-119009, 4430±80 BP). Two other roundwood pieces had possible cut facets on them and two other pieces were charred. Only a length of *c.* 4m had survived marine erosion but there were traces of roundwood fragments in the surface of the clay in a narrow linear band for a distance of *c.* 60m to the south-west and better survival, partially under marine clay, for *c.* 20m to the north-east. Foraminiferal studies show that the feature was built across salt marsh (Gonzalez and Huddart, 2002, p. 582). A very thin, intermittent band of *Phragmites* peat overlying the clay produced a radiocarbon date of 3660–3360 cal BC (Beta-119007, 4750±80 BP). This feature is interpreted as a trackway, an interpretation backed up by other experienced observers (Hibbert pers. comm., Middleton pers. comm.) although it has been queried (B. Coles pers. comm.). Research is continuing into possible alternative interpretations in advance of the final publication but the balance of probability at the moment is that it is does represent a trackway.

LATE MESOLITHIC/NEOLITHIC EXPLOITATION OF THE COASTAL ZONE

Between 9000 to 5000 years BP sea level rise was relatively rapid, from about -20m to about present day sea level, with three major transgressions that reached as far inland as the eastern edge of Downholland Moss at 6980 to 6755, 6500 to 6050 and 5900 to 5615 years BP respectively. A fourth transgressive event occurred between *c.* 4800 and 4554 years BP depositing silts in small embayments at Formby and the Altmouth, but did not inundate significantly the present coastal plain due to the existence of barrier sediments (Tooley 1970; 1978; 1985; Huddart 1992). It is from the Late Mesolithic, therefore, that periods of relatively high sea-level existed and the first real effects were seen in the present coastal areas of West Lancashire, with areas of wetland forming behind the advancing coast-line. To the north of the Altmouth, this resulted in a generally semi-aquatic landscape, with coastal conditions never far away during the marine transgressions of DM I (*c.* 6980–6755 BP) and of DM II (*c.* 6500–6050 BP). With its flanking saltmarsh, this landscape extended into Downholland Moss, as marine transgressions fed from the proto-estuary of the Alt into the basin to the north-east (Figure 2.4a).

It is during DMI that widespread reedswamp and fen carr first formed around the Shirdley Hill Sand ridges near Little Crosby and Ince Blundell to the south, as represented at Flea Moss Wood (Figure 2.4a). The onset of wet conditions in the extreme south of the plain did not occur until the start of the 6th millennium cal BC, in DM III, where the removal of nearby salt marsh conditions after 4730–4490 cal BC (SRR 2699, 5770±50 BP) at Sniggery Wood led to a landscape of reedswamp, freshwater pools and fen carr woodland (Cowell and Innes 1994). The retreat of marine conditions in the coastal strip south of the Alt saw the wetlands becoming drier and more acidic towards the end of the 6th millennium BP. The early and middle Neolithic period in the first half of the 5th millennium BP saw the effects of the marine incursion of DM IV, which is more localised to the area around Hightown and Formby.

As archaeological evidence directly associated with coastal deposits in this region is so limited presently, interpretation of the exploitation of these palaeoenvironments during the

Neolithic has to be seen from evidence within a broader context. This evidence suffers not only from a circumstantial understanding of the physical relationship between the archaeological and palaeoecological evidence, but also from a lack of precision in dating the archaeology, which has to rely on lithic typology. An interpretation based on this evidence, therefore, has to limit itself to identifying general trends within quite broad chronological parameters.

The main evidence occurs to the south of the river Alt, where a number of sites, all surface lithic sites from fieldwalking, occur within *c.* 1km of the present coast (Figure 2.4a), some of which are found either on the edge of the peat/marine clay deposits or on small, sandy dryland islands within them, at heights up to less than 10m OD (Cowell and Innes 1994, chapter 4). The Wirral coastal evidence results from chance finds and excavations conducted in the early 20th century and is found where isolated low cliffs of sandstone or Boulder Clay rise from the coastal plain or lie adjacent to the flanking wetlands (Cowell and Innes 1994, chapter 3).

Most of this material has been ascribed to the Mesolithic, with many flint concentrations containing an element of small blades and debris, with the occasional site including a rare microlith. The occasional earlier Neolithic artefact has been found, limited mainly to stone axes and leaf arrowheads, either as isolated pieces, or very occasionally as part of small discrete flint concentrations, often including blade characteristics, but there is difficulty in identifying a coherent strand of earlier Neolithic lithic evidence in all this material.

On the Sefton coast, the lithic sites mostly exhibit similar characteristics to each other, except for a few relatively large scatters of Late Neolithic/Early Bronze Age date (Figure 2.4a and below). One or two of the larger earlier scatters may represent residential sites, but the majority are small, not very dense and discrete in area, which along with the widespread occurrence of individual blades and blade cores, probably represent small task-sites associated with a mobile system of landuse. These sites all utilise the same local raw material types, which differ from those used in the later Neolithic/Early Bronze Age.

The pollen evidence shows a degree of continuity both in Sefton and on the Wirral, with a pattern of short-lived phases of woodland reduction during the 6th and 5th millennia BP. In the Sefton coastal strip, the pollen site at Flea Moss Wood has cereal-type pollen present in the chronological Late Mesolithic, at *c.* 5900 BP (Cowell and Innes 1994, 84). Flea Moss Wood subsequently shows small-scale woodland reduction in the late Mesolithic with regeneration in the Early Neolithic and significant woodland clearance with evidence of local cereals in the Middle Neolithic. To the south, at Sniggery Wood (Figure 2.4), reasonably significant woodland reduction, associated with ruderal weeds, is seen in episodes prior to and after the elm decline (Cowell and Innes 1994, p. 88).

On the Wirral, a similar occurrence to that at the Sefton site is recorded at Bidston Moss, with early 6th millennium BP cereal-type pollen, followed by repeated small scale, short-term woodland reduction episodes with intervening periods of regeneration. However, the record differs here in that throughout the Early and Middle Neolithic the scale of woodland reduction, while associated with arable weeds and cereal-type pollen, becomes progressively greater, so that by the middle of the 5th millennium BP woodland accounts for only about 20% of total pollen from around the moss (Cowell and Innes 1994, 37–8).

The pollen evidence thus suggests a degree of continuity across the chronological late

6th millennium BP boundary between the Mesolithic and Neolithic periods, with significant changes to these clearance episodes only taking place after *c.* 5000 BP. The differences between the widespread blade-dominated lithic scatters and those of the Late Neolithic imply that, even though certain areas may have been cleared for cereal farming in the first half of the 5th millennium BP, the structure of the settlement pattern may not have changed dramatically during this period. In Sefton, it seems unlikely that all earlier Neolithic sites are buried further to the west beneath the peat and the dunes, so it is a reasonable assumption that some of the sites currently interpreted as Mesolithic may include some from the end of the 6th and earlier 5th millennium BP, their similarity being an expression of the essentially unchanging nature of mobile landuse over the period of the Late Mesolithic and first half of the Neolithic.

Some of these sites lie flanking the wetland in the Alt valley before it reached the proto-estuary, while others lie on sandy dryland soils adjacent to former wetland environments including saltmarsh to the west (Figure 2.4a). Although the relationship between the archaeological and palaeoecological evidence is not precise at the moment, it seems probable that at least some of these sites represent *loci* from where the adjacent marine and flanking wetland environments were exploited in the Late Mesolithic and Early Neolithic.

The evidence on the Northeast part of the Wirral is similar, although without the wider landscape context as in Sefton. The pollen evidence suggests that the repeated visits to the sandstone hills around the wetland flanking the coast at Bidston Moss may have been successively of either a more intensive or extensive nature, with cereal farming becoming a greater component of the landuse during the Early and Middle Neolithic. The New Brighton site at the north-eastern corner of the peninsula appears to have included a relatively high proportion of scrapers, which although not absolutely indicative of date, does suggest that it probably represents more than a short-lived *locus* and can never have been too far from the coast during the late 6th and earlier 5th millennia BP. Although a much more tightly regulated sequence of dates is needed for all classes of evidence, in general terms, it seems as if the increasing woodland clearance is reasonably contemporary with the acidification of the former freshwater wetland areas during the first half of the 5th millennium BP in parts of both Sefton and Wirral (Cowell and Innes 1994, tables 2, 8, 9). Coastal environments and fen wetlands existed in more inundated areas north of the Altmouth in Sefton and on the south-west part of the Wirral coastal plain in the first half of the 5th millennium, with two pollen diagrams from the latter area showing much less evidence of human impact in the vegetational record than those to the north-east in Wirral and Sefton (Cowell and Innes 1994, tables 3, 4). These localities must have still been varied and important areas for coastal and freshwater resources and the pollen and lithic evidence suggests exploitation of them on a mobile basis essentially little different from that in the Mesolithic (Cowell and Innes 1994, 38–43).

In the other areas, around Bidston Moss and Little Crosby, the archaeological evidence suggests mobility is still important at this time but it is tempting to see the loss of freshwater wetlands flanking some parts of the coast south of the Alt to raised bog conditions in the Early-Middle Neolithic as leading to a change in landuse in these areas. Evidence for cereal farming becomes stronger, perhaps compensating for the reduction in resource potential of the former fen and reedswamp areas, exploitation of which kind of environment would have had to shift further north and northwestwards. The degree to which this potential change in landuse may have affected the development of sedentism in the settlement pattern in the former fen wetland areas around Little Crosby is still not clear.

However, direct evidence in this area for exploitation of marine environments at this time, though restricted, does exist in the form of the potential trackway at Hightown. This lay in saltmarsh deposits during the onset of DMIII. It may have afforded a route across wet ground to the inter-tidal area not very far away, where perhaps boats or fishing nets may have been located (Cowell *et al.* in prep). This appears to suggest a degree of planning and co-operation for the exploitation of the tidal reaches of the estuary that could suggest that sedentism may have been a more important element of the landscape in some areas. So far, the archaeological evidence does not bear this out, but if this were the case, then it was only one element within a generally mobile settlement pattern in the Early to Middle Neolithic.

The later Neolithic

The later Neolithic in both the Wirral and Sefton areas saw a relatively prolonged period of low sea-level, in which freshwater peat and subsequently deciduous forest extended beyond the present inter-tidal zone (Figure 2.4a). In Sefton, this is found on the present beach at Hightown, *c.* 800m to the north of the trackway (Figure 2.4a), where a submerged forest peat has radiocarbon dates for its inception after 3520–2930 cal BC (Tooley 1977, 4545±90 BP) while elements of the forest are associated with dates of 3900–2870 cal BC (Beta-119013, 4310±50 BP) and 3090–2660 cal BC (Beta-119012, 4270±60 BP). This evidence is in accord with that from the Hightown structure where the rise of freshwater levels and the accumulation of *Phragmites* peat led to the abandonment of the track after 3660–3360 cal BC (Beta-119007, 4750±80 BP) (Cowell *et al.* in prep). The evidence from the north Wirral coast, to the southwest of the Altmouth, is roughly in accord with this. Pollen and radiocarbon evidence suggests that in general after *c.* 4500 BP forested conditions existed on the present shore until, between *c.* 3900 BP and 3700 BP, water tables rose so that it was replaced by alder and fen carr (Kenna 1986, 13–14), although there is no vegetational evidence for the wider area for this period from Wirral pollen diagrams.

On the Wirral, there is little coherent archaeological evidence during this period. One sherd of pottery is recorded from the beach in the south-west part of the Wirral (Varley 1964), and Late Neolithic transverse arrowheads seem to have come from 19th century collections from the same area. The scatters of Mesolithic/Neolithic flintwork from the low sandstone or Boulder Clay cliffs immediately flanking the present coast are not well recorded enough to know whether they included a later Neolithic element, although they do include barbed and tanged arrowheads and possibly polished stone axes (Cowell and Innes 1994, chapter 3). A midden of bones of aurochs, red deer, boar, dogs and horse from the beach at the northeastern end of the peninsula has a radiocarbon date of 2850–2280 cal BC (Birm-1013, 3980±70 BP) (Kenna 1986).

On the Sefton coast, the lithic evidence from the Little Crosby area (Figure 2.4a) suggests that the nature of the settlements may have changed during the Late Neolithic/ Early Bronze Age, although it is likely that they still represent facets of a mobile system. Flint concentrations of this date are very localised, denser and cover larger areas than the blade-associated assemblages. The surface distribution of the material and the fact that the assemblages consist mainly of a restricted suite of tool-types, with little evidence of on-site flint reduction (Cowell 1991b), suggest it may represent repeated visits to the same location rather than larger, more permanent settlement. The pollen diagram from the adjacent Flea Moss Wood site, however, shows major woodland disturbance with cereal cultivation immediately post-dating 3630–3350 cal BC (SRR-2695, 4670±50 BP), although it is not clear yet if the lithic sites, with their broad potential date range based on typology, are absolutely contemporary with this phase (Cowell and Innes 1994, 85). It does seem, though, that a degree of sedentism had taken place around these sandy ridges in the Late Neolithic. Woodland existed to the west along the present beach and probably on the dryland immediately to the northeast, although the wetland adjacent to the main group of sites on the east had become drier and more acidic by this time. Presumably, with the lower sea level, the fen edge lay further to the north and west, flanking contemporary dunes. These areas could have provided good grazing, perhaps on a seasonal basis, several kilometres from the occupation sites.

The footprints at Formby, *c.* 4km to the north-west, have a less sure relationship to this lithic evidence, as dating of the main print-bearing beds is limited. The radiocarbon date of 2350–1730 cal BC (UB-3869, 3649±109 BP) from alder roots overlying silt beds with footprints at Lifeboat Road is a *terminus ante quem* for the upper set of imprints. Stratigraphically, these occur at a level *c.* 1.5m higher than the lower set of footprints, which suggests the latter could be earlier Neolithic or even Late Mesolithic (Figure 2.2). The upper prints, therefore, could be either contemporary with the Little Crosby late 3rd/ early 2nd millennium BP flint evidence, when coastal effects had retreated in the south of the area, which is perhaps the more likely, or they could belong to the earlier Neolithic period when inter-tidal or estuarine conditions were more widespread along the present coast.

If a Late Neolithic or possibly Early Bronze Age date is accepted for these footprints, then they reinforce the lithic evidence from further south in pointing to a pattern of human mobility in landuse, based on exploiting the intertidal area, as late as the 4th millennium BP. Here, deer, aurochs, cattle and humans made prints in intertidal mud flats, which on-lapped a sandy barrier beach (Huddart *et al.* 1999b). Data relating to stride and footlength in the human prints suggests that women and children's footprints predominate. The flats and flanking reedswamp would be home to wading birds such as crane, whose prints have been found and further out, the presence of marine resources such as shellfish would have been available. Where men's prints have been found, they tend to be associated with red deer tracks, possibly representing hunting episodes (Huddart *et al.* 1999a, 567). Bones of red deer, boar, and *Bos* have been found in the Late Neolithic peat of the submerged forest at Altmouth (Huddart *et al.* 1999a, b).

Unfortunately, the wide belt of high dunes and the presence of Formby to the immediate east of these means that it is not possible to know if similar dryland environments to those in the Little Crosby area occur within *c.* 5 km of the present inter-tidal area. The evidence south of the Alt suggests such areas would have been *foci* of occupation. Alternatively, the whole area may have consisted essentially of varied wetland resources that were exploited from dryland areas further afield, possibly including those areas to the south of the Alt. A freshwater creek may have issued into the inter-tidal zone close to the southern limit of the footprints, at the 'Wicks Wood gap', which it is suggested could have acted as a focus for human settlement (Huddart *et al.* 1999a), although there is no direct archaeological evidence for this and present-day ground conditions militate against easy archaeological survey of the area.

CONCLUSIONS

The evidence required for understanding the general palaeoenvironmental trends in this part of south-west Lancashire and Merseyside is well advanced, much more so than an understanding of the human adaptation to it. The previously strong emphasis on the Mesolithic in this part of the region is now being broadened out, with aspects of the Neolithic landscape and archaeology coming into focus recently. This suggests that patterns of mobility and landuse in relation to exploitation of the coastal zone in some areas subtly change over time during the Neolithic, while in others they remain more constant.

However, much is still unclear. To the north of the Alt, the results from the North West Wetland Survey of South West Lancashire are awaited to illustrate to what extent the settlement pattern of this area can be recreated to aid understanding of its relationship to the palaeo-coastal evidence (Middleton *et al.* in press). To the south of the Alt, a research priority is to clarify the chronology of the lithic assemblages in the area, which will help explain the extent of functional and chronological continuity between sites of the later 6th and earlier 5th millennia BP. Associated with this, is the need for more precise parameters for the chronological sequence of the marine clays and freshwater peats adjacent to the archaeological sites north and west of Little Crosby. Correlation between these two elements would then allow a more confident interpretation of the extent of coastal exploitation during the Late Mesolithic and Early Neolithic periods than is possible presently.

However, with a solid combination of archaeological field survey, palaeoecological background and its attendant interpretation already in place to form the basis for future work on detailed aspects of the evidence, the potential of this area appears high enough for it to contribute significantly to an understanding of Neolithic coastal landuse and settlement patterns over the coming years.

Chapter 3

Wetland–dryland relationships in the Severn Estuary and surroundings during the Mesolithic and Neolithic

Martin Bell

INTRODUCTION

Current orthodoxy has rejected traditional models of the Neolithic that emphasized the transition to farming as the principle cause of social change. Those traditional models also assumed extensive crop husbandry and a sedentary way of life from the Early Neolithic. New models envisage greater continuity from Mesolithic to Neolithic, give less emphasis to the social implications of economic change, suggest that arable agriculture may not have been extensive in some communities and mobile pastoralism was widely practised (Whittle 1999; Thomas 1999). These current views of the Neolithic remain somewhat divergent from what has been envisaged in the interpretation of environmental sequences. Pollen diagrams, even in areas relatively remote from the main concentrations of Neolithic sites, generally show evidence for clearance, albeit often temporary and small-scale, from the Early Neolithic and there is not infrequently some evidence for cereal pollen.

The Severn Estuary wetlands (Figure 3.1a) are flanked by lowlands and surrounding hills; these include extensive areas with calcareous to circum-neutral soils, favourable climate and thus good agricultural potential. This contrasts with the uplands where, particularly in Wales, palynological research was until recently concentrated (*e.g.* Caseldine 1990, figure 11). Mesolithic activity in Wales has a strongly coastal focus, particularly in Pembrokeshire and along the south Wales coast to the Severn Estuary. The distribution of megalithic tombs is very similar to that of coastal Mesolithic sites (compare Lynch *et al.* 2000, figures 1.7 and 2.1). That similarity is further emphasized by the fact that the main inland concentration of Mesolithic sites around the headwaters of the Usk and Wye (which drain into the Severn) occurs in the same general area as the only Welsh inland group of megalithic tombs centred on the Black Mountains. This tomb group is typologically linked to the Severn Cotswold Group (Figure 3.1), the distribution of which is focused on the estuary. The very similar distributions of Mesolithic and Neolithic sites could be argued to suggest a degree of continuity in settlement pattern, economy, or the social significance of place between the Mesolithic and Neolithic.

These relationships raise a number of questions. Were Mesolithic and tomb building communities both reliant to a significant extent on coastal resources? Given rich coastal ecology, were these areas capable of supporting sedentary communities in the Mesolithic? If so did that predispose people towards agriculture, or did it mean that they did not need to adopt domesticates until later than communities in ecologically less favoured areas? The

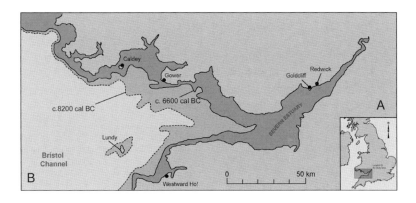

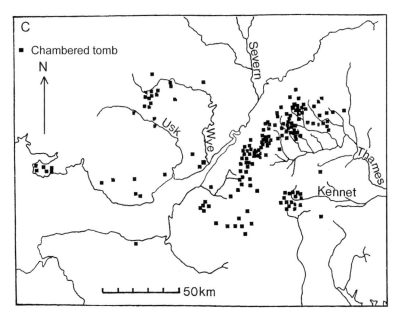

Figure 3.1. The Severn Estuary and Bristol Channel. (a) Location in Britain, arrow marks the Severn Estuary. (b) Coastline in c. 8200 Cal. BC and c. 6600 Cal BC (source Admiralty charts), in relation to the position of selected locations: Caldey; Gower; Goldcliff; Redwick; Westward Ho! (c) Distribution of Neolithic chambered tombs forming the Cotswold-Severn group (Source: Darvill 1982, fig. 2).

exceptional preservation in coastal wetlands provides a context in which it is possible to address these questions. Estuarine sites have the potential to transform our understanding of the period because of the opportunities they provide for comparison of settlement patterns, economy and forms of coastal environmental manipulation on either side of the advent of farming.

The Severn Estuary attracts additional interest as a distinct focus of earlier Neolithic activity represented by the Cotswold-Severn tomb group (Figure 3.1c). The area is northwest of the Wessex chalk, which has seen such a concentration of Neolithic research and on which current models of the period are, to a significant extent, founded. Cooney (2000) has cautioned against the tendency for models of the Neolithic developed in one area, such as Wessex, to be applied wholesale throughout the British Isles and Ireland. Thomas (1999) has likewise questioned the assumption that the Neolithic can be characterised by a homogeneous economic base. The Severn, as a region with an extensive maritime and wetland geographical focus, contrasts with Wessex and provides the opportunity for models developed in the latter to be critically reviewed in the context of a very different landscape.

Research in this study area has suffered from a tendency to 'pigeonhole' and investigate only part of the picture. The Mesolithic and Neolithic have tended to be discussed separately. Furthermore many syntheses have separated the Welsh and English sides and wetland and dryland archaeologies have been discussed in isolation. In the Severn Estuary prehistoric research has so far concentrated more on the Bronze and Iron Ages (Bell *et al.* 2000) and the focus of research is only now shifting to earlier periods (Bell *et al.* 2001, 2002, 2003, forthcoming). Consequently it is not yet possible to formulate a comprehensive model of the Neolithic in the area; the evidence is rather patchy and in some interesting respects contradictory. This paper should be seen as an initial evaluation of the problem, which aims to identify some possible patterns, relationships and research problems which, it is hoped, will help to establish the foundations for targeted future research. Although the focus of the paper is on the Severn Estuary and its surrounding dry ground, selected comparative reference is made to the wealth of evidence from the Somerset Levels and to evidence from the wider region of the Bristol Channel and Pembrokeshire. Calibration of radiocarbon dates has been undertaken using OxCal v3.10 and the curve of Reimer *et al.* (2004); calibrations are given at 2 standard deviations (Bronk Ramsey 1995) and end points have been rounded out after Mook (1986).

MESOLITHIC

The geography of this landscape changed very dramatically during the Mesolithic as a result of sea-level rise (Figure 3.1b). Sea-level curves for the Severn Estuary/Bristol Channel have been prepared by Heyworth and Kidson (1982); a picture now being refined by more detailed site based studies which are adopting more stringent criteria in the selection of sea-level index points to avoid the increasingly recognised effect of peat autocompaction (Allen 1999). Recent detailed studies include the Axe Valley (Haslett *et al.* 1998), Porlock (Jennings *et al.* 1998) and Goldcliff (Bell *et al.* 2000). Figure 3.1b plots the position of the coast at mean high water spring tide using the curves of Heyworth and Kidson (1982; Bell *et al.* 2000, figure 17.2). It is based on Admiralty Hydrographic charts; the map does not therefore take account of subsequent erosion and deposition. However, at the scale represented, and at the time slices shown, it is considered that this provides an adequate general impression of broad-scale coastal change.

At *c.* 8200 cal BC sea-level stood at *c.* -35m OD and the mouth of the river Severn, not at this stage a fully formed estuary, was off Gower about 80km west of its present position. With the rapid sea-level rise of the early Holocene, the estuary migrated upstream to the east and by *c.* 6600 cal BC the head of the estuary was off Minehead and by *c.* 5600 cal BC sea-level stood at *c.* -4m OD (Bell *et al.* 2000). Early Mesolithic coastal sites will have been inundated by the Holocene sea-level rise, but sites of the later Mesolithic are preserved in the intertidal zone at Westward Ho!, north Devon *c.* 5900–4800 cal BC (Balaam *et al.* 1987, table 1) and Goldcliff *c.* 5300–5660 cal BC (Bell *et al.* 2000, figure 4.13); several other sites are known in the intertidal zone in Pembrokeshire (Lewis 1992; Bell 2000). The Goldcliff site is on the flanks of a former bedrock island. The main activities seem to have been the utilisation of lithic raw materials from estuarine gravels, the hunting of deer and pigs and fishing. Very abundant deer footprint-tracks, in particular, within the lower Wentlooge sedimentary formation of the Severn Estuary (Allen 1997) demonstrate the abundance of animals within the coastal wetland. Footprint-tracks of people at Uskmouth, Magor and Goldcliff (Aldhouse-Green *et al.* 1992; Bell *et al.* 2001) mark expeditions out onto the coastal mudflats by groups from Goldcliff or similar sites. Saltmarshes, reed swamps and fen communities will also have provided valued resources at this time, although in these environments the survival of footprint-tracks will be less frequent and more localised than in mudflats.

The concentration of Mesolithic sites in coastal areas, in which marine and estuarine resources were abundant, might suggest the possibility of sedentary Mesolithic occupation as in coastal areas of Scandinavia (Andersen 1995). However, this hypothesis is not sustained by the existing evidence. At Goldcliff the lithic assemblage has few tools and is not suggestive of the diverse activities that would be associated with a permanent home-base settlement. The other known sites, although studied in less detail also seem to lack the concentrations, or range, of artifact types that might point to sedentism. Where artifacts are abundant (*e.g.* at The Nab Head, Pembrokeshire) the evidence seems to suggest visits to 'persistent places' (Barton *et al.* 1995) over long periods rather than permanent settlements.

The group of inland and upland sites around the headwaters of rivers notably the Usk and Wye which drain into the Severn Estuary has already been noted. Upland sites have been investigated below blanket peat at Waun-Fignen-Felen (Smith and Cloutman 1988; Barton *et al.* 1995), where short-lived hunting-related activities took place beside a former lake between *c.* 9300–6000 radiocarbon years BP (*c.* 8600–4800 cal BC). Use of beach flint and Greensand chert for artifacts indicates that this seasonal upland activity was related to movement, perhaps up the river valleys from the Bristol Channel and Severn Estuary (Barton *et al.* 1995, figure 6). Short-term use of the Wye Valley caves during both the Upper Palaeolithic and Mesolithic may well have been associated with such seasonal movements. The small quantity and low diversity of artifact types is again suggestive of transitory seasonal use, or hunting camps (*e.g.* King Arthur's Cave, ApSimon *et al.* 1992), rather than sedentary occupation. Mesolithic artifacts are associated with marine shells of cowrie (*Trivia monacha*) at Madawg Cave and cowrie and periwinkle (*Littorina* sp) in King Arthur's cave (Barton 1994; 1996). A Mesolithic assemblage from a terrace of the Usk at Gwernvale includes lithic evidence of both early and later Mesolithic date and also an Upper Palaeolithic flint industry (Britnell and Savory 1984). In this case, the coincidence of occupation, over an extended period, is not readily explained by an obvious topographic feature (*e.g.* a cave). Perhaps habitual use of specific paths, associated with frequented routes of seasonal movement, and the creation of disturbed areas, particularly perhaps at path intersection places, played an important role in structuring the pattern of settlement over very extended timescales (Bell 2003).

On the English side the main concentration of Mesolithic activity near the coast is on the sandy Burtle Beds of the Somerset Levels and this dates mainly to ninth to seventh millennia cal BC with a lack of Late Mesolithic evidence from the period of maximum marine transgression (Coles 1989, 14; Brown 1986, 25). On the Severn Estuary English shore there are coastal sites at Oldbury (Allen 1998) and Blackstone Rocks, Clevedon (Sykes 1938) and a site near the wetland edge has recently been excavated at Birdcombe (Gardiner 2000). The main concentrations of Mesolithic sites are, however, in upland locations on the Cotswolds (Saville 1984, figure 4) and the Mendips (Norman 1982, figure 3.2).

It is notable that several caves around the Severn Estuary and South Wales have produced burials dated to the Mesolithic. Caves with burials include Aveline's Hole, which contained perhaps as many as 70 individuals (Smith 1992b), Gough's Cave and Totty Pot on Mendip (Gardiner 2000), several caves on Gower and on Caldey Island (Aldhouse-Green 2000, 37). Dating of these burials does not, however, fit a model of an evolutionary trend towards coastal sedentism with burial, which has been proposed more widely in Atlantic Europe (Cunliffe 2001, 138). Two of the Mendip sites are dated to the early Mesolithic (Aveline's Hole 8580–7970 cal BC (OxA-799, 9100±100BP); Gough's Cave, 8650–7780 cal BC (OxA-150, 9080±150BP)) and were in use at a time when the sea was *c.* 100km west of Mendip (Figure 3.1B). Isotopic evidence shows that marine resources did not contribute to the diet of the Aveline's Hole community, demonstrating that their seasonal round did not extend to the Bristol Channel (Schulting and Richards 2000). Conversely, burials in the Caldey Caves, which were close to the contemporary coast, show isotopic evidence for the use of marine resources. A later Mesolithic individual from Fox Hole, Gower, also on the coast, by contrast had a largely terrestrial diet (Aldhouse-Green 2000, 27; Richards 2000).

The very early Holocene dates of some burials make it possible that the origins of these burial practices lie, not in an evolutionary development within the Mesolithic, but in the Upper Palaeolithic. Burials at Aveline's Hole include beads made from pig and red deer incisors and the use of red ochre (Smith 1992 a and b), practices reminiscent of the necklace of pierced shells and the use of red ochre in Upper Palaeolithic burial of the 'Red Lady' of Paviland, Gower (Aldhouse-Green 2000). However, Britain was unoccupied during the last glacial maximum (Housley *et al.* 1997). Thus this hypothesis depends on late glacial colonisation by a group that had retreated south during the glacial maximum and later returned, exhibiting some similar cultural traits but under very different environmental circumstances.

Waun-Fignen-Felen has produced well-documented evidence for the impact of fire on both woodland and heath species at the upland woodland edge *c.* 6600–4360 cal BC (Smith and Cloutman 1988). There are also extensive charcoal spreads in coastal contexts at Goldcliff (5200–5700 cal BC; Bell *et al.* 2000, figure 4.13; Bell *et al.* 2002), associated with the Mesolithic midden site at Westward Ho! in the Bristol Channel (*c.* 5800–5000 cal BC; Balaam *et al.* 1987, table 1) and in a non-settlement context at Redwick, 6380–6050 cal BC (Beta-134639, 7330±70 BP, Allen and Bell 1999; Bell *et al.* 2001). There is also evidence for disturbance of woodland at the wetland edge at Vurlong Reen *c.* 4000–4300 cal BC (Walker *et al.* 1998). Druce (1998) has also found charcoal associated with intertidal peats at Burnham-on-Sea dated to 4350–4040 cal BC (Wk-5299, 5370±70BP). The possibility must be considered that people were exploiting open areas created by natural disturbance factors such as storms and wildfire (Brown 1997). However, the considerable difficulty of burning natural woodland (Rackham 1986), particularly in damp coastal wetlands, and the association between evidence of burning and lithic scatters at Waun-Fignen-Felen, Goldcliff, Westward Ho! and some of the Pembrokeshire sites (Lewis 1992), strongly suggest that Mesolithic communities were transforming the coastal woodland edge by burning. Such practices are widely attested in the British uplands where they are presumed to represent a strategy to increase the biomass of plant resources and deer (Simmons 1996). A model of Mesolithic environmental relations (Simmons 2001, plate 5) assumes that burning was localised in upland and lake edge situations but did not occur on the coast. Situations where direct comparison can be made between upland and lowland Mesolithic ways of life, environmental relationships and impacts are rare. Such comparison is possible in the Severn and it is of particular interest that burning should have occurred at both the coastal and upland woodland edges of hypothetical seasonal territories linked by axial movements up the river valleys. The possibility is suggested that the concentration of Mesolithic activity on the coast is not purely a reflection of an abundance of marine resources but also reflects a diverse mosaic of environment types created by a range of disturbance factors, which included human agency (as a cause of fire) but would also have involved the effects of storms, floods and grazing animals. Coastal factors would have created landscape mosaics of exceptional variety and dynamism, much more so than the woodland edge in the upland. It is therefore notable to find significant evidence for fire in lowland contexts. The Mesolithic coastal environment and the relative importance and interaction between the spectrum of disturbance factors is a subject of current research (see concluding section below).

NEOLITHIC ACTIVITY ON DRYLAND

Figure 3.2 shows the distribution of Neolithic sites and findspots on dryland surrounding the Severn Estuary Levels. The geographical/administrative areas included have each been the subject of surveys of Neolithic archaeology. These include maps of site and artifact distributions that have been combined to produce this map. Neolithic sites in Wales were mapped by Savory (1980, figure 5.2) and more recently by Lynch (2000, figure 2.1). Use has also been made of a recent survey of lithic evidence from south Wales (Locock 2000), from which all axes and sites with more than 20 lithic artifacts have been plotted. Neolithic sites in Gloucestershire have been mapped by Darvill (1984, figures 1, 3 and 7), and the Neolithic axes of the Cotswolds have been published and mapped by Tyler (1976). Maps in Darvill (1984) suggest a complete absence of evidence from the Forest of Dean; however, there are a number of finds of polished axes (marked on Figure 3.2) and field walking by local groups has produced several Neolithic lithic scatters (Walters 1992) which are not marked on Figure 3.2 because sufficiently precise location details are not known. Sites in the former County of Avon have been mapped by Darvill (1986, figures 2.1, 2.4 and 2.10) and in Somerset, including north Somerset south of the Bristol Avon, by Minnitt (1982, figure 4.2). Each of these surveys has been prepared at different dates over 20 years so there will be contrasts in the completeness of coverage and the approaches adopted in the administrative regions on which the map is based.

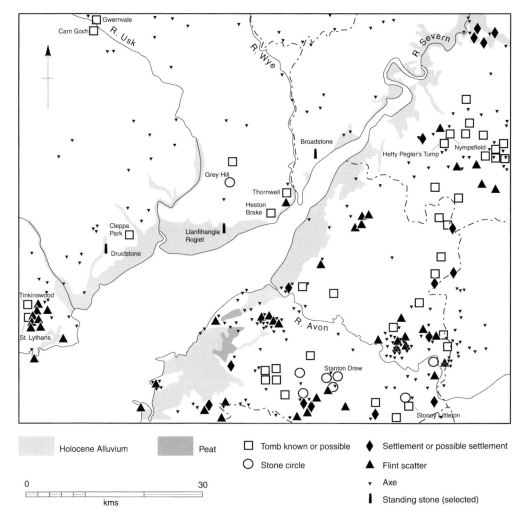

Figure 3.2. The distribution of Neolithic sites and findspots on dryland surrounding the Severn Estuary (for sources used see text).

    The distributions in Figure 3.2 will also be influenced by the location of past field projects and the favoured areas of particularly active collectors. In the case of lithic finds in particular, the distribution of disturbance factors, particularly arable, which may bring finds to light, is an additional factor. An obvious observation is that there is less evidence of Neolithic activity on the Welsh than the English side of the Severn Estuary. This may in part be a result of the foregoing factors: there is less arable and has been a much less active history of prehistoric research by both amateurs and professional archaeologists on the Welsh side. Even so, Figures 3.1 and 3.2 show extensive evidence for Neolithic activity around the Severn Estuary and the implications of this require particular consideration. The area is the focus of the Cotswold-Severn Neolithic tomb group (Darvill 1982), (Figure 3.1). The similarities of construction method and burial practice, which exist within this

Tomb	OD Ht	Distance to estuary
Thornwell Farm	50m	*c.* 300m
Heston Brake	30m	*c.* 300m
Cleppa Park	40m	*c.* 1500m

Table 3.1 Locations of chambered tombs close to the Severn Estuary in South Wales.

group, point to a commonality of belief, or purpose, among communities on both sides of the estuary, which are likely to have been united (rather than divided) by the communication possibilities that the estuary offered. The distribution of tombs also suggests commun-ication, or population movement, west along the coast to Gower and north up the river valleys to the Black Mountains group at the headwaters of the Usk and Wye, an area which, it has already been suggested, was the focus of seasonal movements during the Mesolithic. Tilley (1994) has argued that the setting and form of tombs often acknowledge and seems to reflect natural landscape features that may have been of significance in relation to the seasonal movements of Mesolithic communities, their significance being reworked in the Neolithic by monument construction.

The main concentration of Neolithic sites is on the limestone of the Cotswolds and Mendip where Neolithic tombs mostly occur above the 120m contour (Darvill 1984) and are mostly some kilometres inland from the Estuary. On the Welsh side there are fewer tombs but there are three at lower elevations and directly overlooking the nearby estuary (Table 3.1). Distances given are those to the edge of the present levels. In parts of the estuary this corresponds to its Neolithic limits because there is quite a marked break of slope, due in part to the existence of an earlier Ipswichian Interglacial shoreline (Allen 2001). However, in the case of the vicinity of these three tombs there is no specific evidence of the position of the Neolithic estuary edge, which might have been somewhat further than the present levels edge. Even so, they would all have been close to the levels and have overlooked the wetland.

As regards structures of possible domestic function there is evidence from Wales as a whole, for structures somewhat comparable to those increasingly being found in Ireland (Lynch 2000, figure 2.2). Around the Severn Estuary Neolithic wood structures have been found associated with possible small-scale domestic occupation below both of the chambered tombs which have been the subject of recent scientific excavation at Gwernvale (Britnell and Savory 1984) and Hazleton (Saville 1990), at both of which earlier Mesolithic activity also occurred. Thomas (1988) prefers to see this as evidence of previous use for ritual and exchange rather than settlement. There are also hints of wood structures below some of the tombs subject to earlier excavations, such as Sales Lot (Darvill 1982, 11). Other wood structures occur within the Crickley Hill causewayed enclosure (Dixon 1994). Rather more difficult to interpret are early finds of possible rectangular structures in south Wales beyond the mapped area: one of Middle Neolithic date from Mount Pleasant in the Vale of Glamorgan (Lynch 2000) and two Late Neolithic examples in the Glamorgan uplands at Cefn Glas (Clayton and Savory 1990) and Cefn Cisanws (Savory 1980). Although not all of these structures are necessarily domestic it would be rash to conclude, given this evidence from the small number of south Welsh Neolithic sites excavated, that these communities lived mainly in tents and followed a largely mobile lifestyle.

Other evidence of settlements is limited. Possible examples were indicated on the county maps on which Figure 3.2 is based because for instance of the presence of features containing artifacts, *e.g.* at Gloucester (Darvill 1987) and Chew Valley (Minnitt 1982). Particular concentrations of flint scatters may also indicate settlement locations, although Thomas (1999) has cautioned against the simple equation of lithic scatters with settlement, some may just represent the sites of flint working.

Given the evidence from Hazleton and Gwernvale, the relationship between lithic scatters and tombs in parts of Figure 3.2 encourages the view that other tombs lay close to areas of domestic activity (Darvill 1982, 82). For instance, on the Welsh side of the estuary there is a Neolithic flint and pottery scatter close to the recently discovered Thornwell Farm tomb (Hughes 1996; Maylan 1991) and a very pronounced concentration of lithic scatters occurs in the Wenvoe area near the Tinkinswood, St Lythans and Coed y Cwm tombs at the western edge of the mapped area, the last just off the map (Locock 2000; Owen-John 1988).

Axe finds are numerous and widely scattered, including areas of south Wales well beyond tombs and lithic scatters. Concentrations of axe finds on the English side occur in association with the densest concentrations of lithic scatters. There is also a tendency, particularly on the English side and around Cardiff, for axe finds to occur in greater numbers close to the wetland. Allen (1990) also notes examples on the English side.

Figure 3.2 presents a composite picture for the whole Neolithic. Those tombs that have been dated are essentially earlier Neolithic, most dates being *c.* 3780–2900 cal BC (Whittle and Wysocki 1998, table 13). The main later Neolithic sites are concentrated in the upland areas in which the earlier tombs were also located. These include the recently identified great timber circle at Stanton Drew and the stone circles which, to judge by sequences elsewhere, succeed it (Pitts 2000), and the other Mendip circles and the henge at Condicot (east of the mapped area) The stone circle at Grey Hill, Wales may be either Late Neolithic or earlier Bronze Age. If the distribution of those flint assemblages with diagnostic earlier and later Neolithic artifact scatters are compared (Thomas 1991, figures 2.1–2.3), there is little evidence for the utilisation beyond the limestone of a wider range of geologies, lowland and river valley locations which Thomas' maps indicate elsewhere in his central southern England study area. Exceptions are possible evidence for later Neolithic settlement in the Severn valley at Gloucester and Tewkesbury (Darvill 1984, figure 7), but there is at present little indication of greater Late Neolithic activity on the lowlands surrounding the Severn Estuary itself.

ENVIRONMENTAL EVIDENCE ON DRYLAND

Two Cotswold-Severn tombs excavated under modern scientific conditions produced good environmental evidence: Hazleton (Saville 1990) and Ascott-under-Wychwood (Evans 1972). In each case the evidence is consistent with the site having a history of pre-tomb activity involving earlier clearance and at Hazleton possible cultivation. After monument construction, regeneration occurred within the ditch sediments at both tombs. A single mollusc sample from an Old Land Surface below the putative tomb at Druid Stoke had a mainly woodland fauna (Bell in Smith 1989). Two later Neolithic henges have produced environmental evidence. On Mendip one of the Priddy henges was constructed in grassland (Dimbleby in Tratman 1967) and on the Cotswolds at Condicot mollusc evidence is from post-construction ditch fills and is of shade-loving character, suggesting that the monument was not created in a fully cleared landscape and that regeneration occurred soon after (Bell in Saville 1983). Although the evidence is limited it would seem to indicate that Neolithic clearance on the Cotswolds was less extensive and of shorter duration than in those areas of Wessex with the greatest concentration of Neolithic activity (Bell 1987).

WETLAND PERSPECTIVES

Archaeological evidence

The distribution of wetland sites is shown in Figure 3.3 and provides a complementary perspective to the dry land picture of Figure 3.2. Wetland archaeological evidence is contained within a Holocene sedimentary sequence that has been well documented by Allen (*e.g.* 1987; 1997; Allen and Rae 1987). Within this sequence Neolithic evidence comes from the following types of context: –

(i)   Essentially dryland sites on old land surfaces that became subject to marine influence during the Neolithic, or later.

(ii)   Peat deposits representing reed swamp, fen woodland or raised bog environments which formed extensively in the wetland during the Neolithic and Bronze Age and represent the major source of pollen evidence from the study area.

(iii)   Minerogenic silts which represent marine transgressive episodes separating the main phases of peat formation and also fill the palaeochannels which dissect the wetland.

The most significant concentration of Neolithic material so far identified is from the wetland margins at Oldbury where some material is from a pre-inundation landsurface, some is *in situ* on sandy silt of estuarine origin and some has been found transposed on the foreshore (Allen 1990; 1998). 81 pieces of Neolithic flint are reported including polished axes, scrapers, knives and arrowheads, a range suggestive of diverse activities and thus of more than transitory occupation, particularly because pits, postholes and hearths have been found. Evidence has been found for cattle, deer and possibly human footprints at this site. Charcoal has been radiocarbon dated to 4330–3980 cal BC (Beta-84850, 5310±70 BP). A polished axe and worked flints are likewise known in transposed contexts at Hills Flats (Allen 1990). On the Welsh side of the estuary there are a few flint flakes associated with a charcoal horizon dated to 3330–2670 cal BC (SWAN-133, 4320±80BP) in peat on the edge of Goldcliff island, a few flints from Neolithic alder carr peat near the wetland edge at Vurlong Reen (Ferris and Dingwall 1992, 8; Parkhouse and Lawler 1990, 9), a polished axe of rhyolite unstratified from the intertidal zone at Magor (Green 1989, figure 4), a probable leaf arrowhead from Rumney (Fulford *et al.* 1994) and several Neolithic artifacts reworked in a Bronze Age palaeochannel fill at Caldicot (Nayling and Caseldine 1997). Small Neolithic assemblages are similarly associated with wetland edge contexts at Blackstone Rocks, Clevedon (Sykes 1938) and Brean Down where there is also a radiocarbon date of 3790–3080 cal BC (Har-7023, 4720 ±140BP, Bell 1990). Polished axes come from peats exposed in dock construction at Cardiff and Barry Docks and

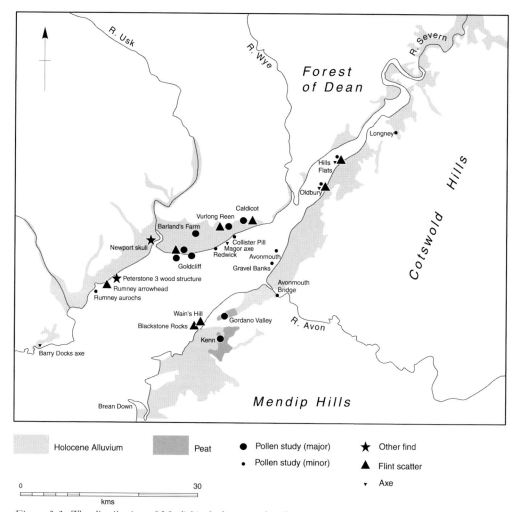

Figure 3.3. The distribution of Neolithic findspots and pollen sequences in the Severn Estuary wetland (for details of pollen sites see Table 3.2).

further west in the Bristol Channel an axe in its birchwood haft was found on the foreshore at Aberavon (Savory 1971). Some of the older finds of Neolithic axes plotted on Figure 3.2 (*e.g.* after Tyler 1976) are also from locations that suggest they were from within, or close to, the wetland. Allen (1990) notes some examples.

It is noteworthy that four of the sites mentioned here have evidence of both Mesolithic and Neolithic activity, *i.e.* Blackstone Rocks, Oldbury, Goldcliff, and Caldicot. How much significance should be attached to this is unclear because the first three are rocky promontories in wetland and the fourth (Caldicot) on the edge of a river channel, all topographic situations which are inherently likely to have attracted repeated use without necessarily having to infer continuity of activities.

The lithic finds show that there was some activity in the wetland, but most of the finds

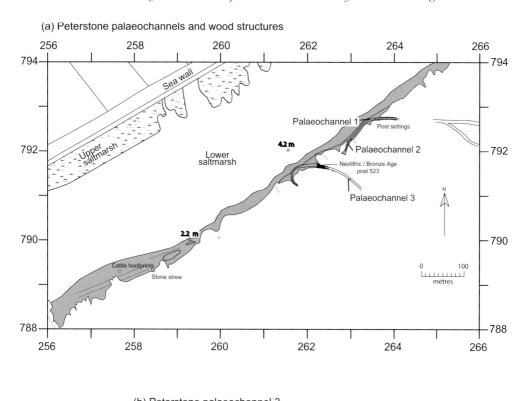

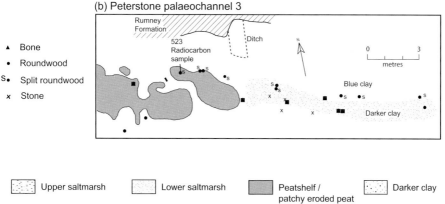

Figure 3.4. Peterstone, Severn Estuary: (a) plan of palaeochannels of the Neolithic and Bronze Age (b) palaeochannel 3 with a wood stake dated to the Late Neolithic or Early Bronze Age.

are close to the wetland edge rather than at the heart of the wetland. Isolated flint axes and arrowheads could derive from expeditions for hunting, or the acquisition of raw materials in wetland. They might equally reflect ritual wetland deposition; Allen (1998) records that the Oldbury axes and a later barbed and tanged arrowhead from Hills Flats may have been ritually broken.

There is limited further evidence of specialist activities in the wetland from wood
structures. At Peterstone a number of palaeochannels have been identified in the intertidal
zone (Figures 3.3 and 3.4; Bell *et al.* 2000, 304–307). Palaeochannels of this type, which
occur widely in the Severn Estuary, are of archaeological interest because a number of
examples, including three of the four Peterstone channels are associated with evidence of
wood structures. Palaeochannel 3 was 1–2m wide and was traced for about 120m. Twenty
posts, six bones and four stones were recorded along the exposed length under mud-free
conditions in March 1996. A more detailed survey of the landward 19m of channel was
carried out under more muddy conditions in March 1997. This recorded eight posts aligned
roughly along the north side of the channel; six bones and four stones were also identified.
One of these posts (523) was excavated; it was a worked timber of square section the end
of which had been pointed by many axe blows. The timber has been dated to 2570–2200
cal BC (GrN-24149, 3910±60BP). It is of particular note as the earliest wood structure so
far identified in the Severn Estuary dating to the Late Neolithic or Early Bronze Age. The
channel fill is clearly partly eroded; some of the verticals are outside the channel and were
clearly driven into its bank from a higher level. Lines of roundwood posts parallel with
channel edges form part of a later prehistoric fishing structure at Cold Harbour Pill (Bell
et al. 2000, figure 16.9) and it seems probable that the Peterstone structure is related in
some way to fishing. Another of the Peterstone palaeochannels contains wood structures,
one of which is dated to the Middle Bronze Age, and another contains Middle Bronze Age
sherds. This points to activity, probably related to fishing, extending over a period of about
a millennium. On the English side of the Estuary at Kenn a worked wooden stake, of
probable Neolithic or Early Bronze Age date, points to some sort of wetland activity
(Gilbertson and Hawkins 1983; Butler 1988) although given the number of isolated pieces
of worked wood from the Somerset Levels (Coles 1984) this is not necessarily a trackway
as originally hypothesized.

Neolithic evidence from within the Severn Estuary wetlands appears to be very limited
by comparison with what we have seen in the surrounding uplands and is particularly
modest by comparison with the Somerset Levels just to the south. Here 30 trackways and
many stray finds are known from the Neolithic. These span the entire period and although
they were mostly very short-lived (10–15 years at most) a recent analysis of their
chronological distribution indicates that there is only one century in the Neolithic without
evidence for trackway construction (Coles and Coles 1998). Here artifact concentrations
and the focal points of trackway convergence point to the possible locations of Neolithic
dryland settlements (Coles and Coles 1998). The density of finds overall is a 'strong
indication of wetland dependence rather than wetland passage' (Coles 1989, 23). On present
evidence it must be assumed that the Somerset Levels wetland, which by the Neolithic
period would have been freshwater dominated and with many bedrock and sand ridges and
islands mostly less than 2–3km from dry land, was for Neolithic communities a more
attractive habitat than the part of the Severn Estuary levels presently exposed in the
intertidal zone, much of it 4 to 6 km from bedrock and during the Neolithic subject to
greater marine influence. Even on the dryland fringes of the Somerset Levels, however,
flint scatters of Neolithic date are few compared to the much greater evidence of Mesolithic
activity (Coles 1989).

Other evidence for Neolithic activity in coastal wetland comes from the Taw- Torridge

No	Site	NGR	Start date (¹⁴Cyrs BP)	Start date (Cal BC)	End date (¹⁴Cyrs BP)	End Date (Cal BC)	Sampling interval ^{14}C yrs	Reference
1	Rumney aurochs	ST 2294 7745	4060±70 BP (Car-851)	2880–2460	-		-	Walker in Green 1989
2	Goldcliff Pit 15	ST 3692 8202	5920±80BP (Car-1501)	5000–4580	3640±60BP (Car-1499)	2200–1820	c70yrs	Caseldine 2000
3	Goldcliff Hill Farm Pond	ST 3708 8213	4320±80BP (SWAN-133)	3350–2650	3180±70BP (SWAN-104)	1620–1260		Caseldine 2000
4	Goldcliff East	ST 3786 8220	5950±80BP (Car-659)	5050–4610	3130±70BP (Car-644)	1530–1210	c35yrs	Smith and Morgan 1989 Bell forthcoming
5	Barlands' Farm	ST 405 864	5920±50BP (Beta-72511)	4940–4680	2900±60BP (Beta-72506)	1290–910	c58yrs	Walker et al. 1998
6	Vurlong Reen	ST 452 873	5740±70BP (Beta-63595)	4780–4400	2470±60BP (Beta-63590)	780–400	c68yrs	Walker et al. 1998
7	Redwick	ST 4244 8372	-	-	-	-	-	De Volder 1998 Caseldine in prep
8	Collister Pill	ST 4527 8550	-	-	-	-	-	Burbridge 1998
9	Caldicot	ST 488 886	4670±80BP (Car-1323)	3650–3100	2400±70BP (Car-1405)	780–370		Nayling and Caseldine 1997
10	Longney	SO 766 116	5090BP?	c3900	2830BP ?	c980	-	Brown 1982, 1987
11	Oldbury	ST 5984 9441–ST 6018 9369	6490±90BP (Wk-7329)	5620–5300	3930±160BP (Wk-7327)	2900–1950	-	Druce 2000 Brown 2005
12	Avonmouth M5 bridge	cS277	4305±100 BP (no lab no)	3350–2550	-	-	-	Gilbertson et al. 1990
13	Avonmouth Gravel banks	cST 5282	7150±70BP (Wk-5826)	6210–5840	6460±70BP (Wk-5860)	5540–5300	-	Druce 2000
14	Gordano valley	ST 436 729	11020±190BP (SRR-3203)	11600–10600	3820±100BP (SRR-3199)	2600–1950	c144yrs	Gilbertson et al. 2000
15	Kenn	ST 430 680	6100±100BP (no lab no)	5300–4750	3510±100BP (no lab no)	2150–1500	-	Butler 1998

Table 3.2 Pollen sites of Neolithic date in the Severn Estuary Wetlands. For locations, see Figure 3.3

Estuary at Westward Ho! (Balaam *et al.* 1987), where an intertidal peat surface revealed two rows of wooden posts dated to 3780–3370 cal BC (HAR-5642, 4840±70 BP). What these represent is uncertain, perhaps a truncated trackway, or fishtrap. In either case the find represents a continued interest in estuarine resources a millennium later than the Mesolithic shell midden and this continuing estuarine interest is further reinforced by the discovery of both Mesolithic and Neolithic flints on the site of the Yelland stone row in the same estuary (Rogers 1946).

Caves, burial and questions of diet

The practice of burial in caves noted above in the Mesolithic continues in this area into the Neolithic with dated examples in the Bristol Channel-Severn Estuary area from Little Hoyle, Pembrokeshire; Spurge Hole Cave, Gower; King Arthur's Cave, Forest of Dean; Haywood Cave and Charterhouse Warren Cave on Mendip (Richards and Hedges 1999; Levitan and Smart 1989). There are also hints of a possible relationship between interments in caves and those in chambered tombs. The bone assemblage in the Parc le Breos, Gower tomb contained some very old animal bones radiocarbon dated to the upper Palaeolithic to middle Mesolithic, the condition of which suggests they had previously been in a cave environment (Whittle and Wysocki 1998, 177).

Deposition of human skulls in wetlands is well attested at Goldcliff in the Bronze Age (Bell *et al.* 2000, chapter 5). This practice may have had Neolithic origins. At Alexandra Docks, Newport a human skull was found in 1910 at *c.* -9m OD. The original report (Keith 1911) records a sheep metatarsal from a level below the skull and finds of flints, of which no record was kept. The skull has recently been dated to 2860–2390 cal BC (OxA-7656, 3995±45 BP). Deposition was in gravel, therefore presumably in a Neolithic channel of the Ebbw/Usk, which today have their confluence within 400m of the findspot. Given the riverine/wetland location of this find it is striking that stable isotope data showed that the individual had not obtained a significant dietary contribution from marine sources. Although this is just one individual, it is consistent with isotopic evidence from all the other Neolithic individuals so far examined from south Wales: 10 individuals in the Parc le Breos tomb, Gower just 2km from the coast (Whittle and Wysocki 1998), three Early Neolithic individuals from Caldey Island and a burial from Little Hoyle Cave, Tenby (Schulting and Richards 2000). None of these obtained a significant proportion of their diet from marine sources. The implication is of a radical shift away from marine resources early in the Neolithic. A less plausible hypothesis is that the remains of individuals from inland areas were transported to the coast for interment.

Given the extent to which dating and isotopic studies of human remains in this area have transformed our understanding of its Mesolithic and Neolithic archaeology it is particularly desirable that these methods are also applied to other human skeletal finds of appropriate date. An example is the six human crania and other bones found in 1909 on a ledge, presumably from a part-destroyed cave or rock shelter, in Ifton Quarry which is 1km from the edge of the estuary and 1km from Caldicot (Anwyl 1909; Knowles 1911), R. Schulting (pers. comm.) currently has the analysis of these finds in hand.

Palaeoenvironmental evidence

Palaeoenvironmental evidence from the estuary is synthesised by Bell (2001). Bennett's (1989) map of dominant woodland types, *c.* 3780 cal BC shows alder woods on the Severn and Somerset wetlands flanked by lime woods with ash woods on the Cotswolds to the east. This general picture can now be elaborated using 15 pollen diagrams (Table 3.2), which are dated with varying levels of precision to the Neolithic. These diagrams are in agreement that within the wetland alder and birch dominated the woods. A plan of one such area of Late Mesolithic woodland has been made at Goldcliff (Bell *et al.* 2000, figure 4.2). Lime was a major constituent of woods on the dry ground at Longney, Vurlong Reen, Cardiff East Moors, Gordano Valley and ICI Avonmouth. The importance of lime *c.* 5000 BP on dry ground surrounding the levels, as in much of lowland Britain, has been demonstrated by Greig (1982). On most of the other sites the woodland was dominated by oak, *e.g.* Caldicot, Barland's Farm, the Rumney aurochs site, Redwick and Goldcliff.

At the well-dated sites of appropriate age the elm decline *c.* 3800 cal BC is represented and at most sites evidence of human activity has been claimed at this time and subsequently. The most detailed investigation has been of changes on the small former bedrock island at Goldcliff (Smith and Morgan 1987; Caseldine 2000):-

(i)   Palynological evidence for a classic landnam episode directly following the elm decline *c.* 3800 cal BC with pastoral activity followed by some cereal pollen and mixed farming, the whole lasting *c.* 260 calendar years before regeneration. But see Dark (forthcoming) for a critique of the Landnam interpretation.

(ii) A charcoal layer at the base of a peat at the wetland margin (Bell *et al.* 2000, figure 3.7) dated to 3330–2670 cal BC (Swan-133, 4320±80BP).

(iii) A second charcoal layer on the top of the same peat dated to 1620–1290 cal BC (Swan-104, 3180±70BP, Bell *et al.* 2000, figure 3.7). The radiocarbon date is identical to that previously obtained by Smith and Morgan (1987) for the *Tilia* decline and agriculture at Goldcliff East.

A low level of small-scale and temporary Neolithic agricultural activity is also indicated by the pollen diagrams at Caldicot (Nayling and Caseldine 1997) and Kenn (Butler 1988). At Barland's Farm open country taxa also appear during the Neolithic but there are no cereals and activity seems to have been pastoral (Walker *et al.* 1998). Gordano Valley is a narrow valley surrounded by dryland. Here a two-stage elm decline occurs but there is no clear evidence of anthropogenic impact until much later in prehistory (Gilbertson *et al.* 1990). Some of the diagrams from the heart of the wetland show little sign of clearance or anthropogenic effects in the Neolithic, but this is not surprising because they would have been distant from dry ground.

The limitations of our chronological resolution should, however, be acknowledged. There are five diagrams in which available dates enable the calculation of the average sampling interval during the Neolithic in terms of radiocarbon years (Table 3.2). These intervals range from 35 (Goldcliff East) to 144 years (Gordano Valley). Coles (2000) has argued that many Neolithic settlement sites in Britain and Europe, in common with the Sweet Track, may have lasted no more than 15–20 years. It follows that the present level of chronological resolution may be missing, or blurring, some phases of Neolithic activity. The overall picture is of generally short-lived Neolithic clearance followed by regeneration. Although the pattern of activity is somewhat similar to the Somerset Levels the evidence for clearance on the estuary margins is more limited and the duration of clearance episodes shorter than that documented in the Somerset Levels. Here comparisons of pollen spectra from various sites have led to the identification of patterns of clearance and regeneration that are coeval over the area of investigation. Initial clearance between 3800–3100 cal BC was followed by regeneration and further clearance from 2800–2200 cal BC (Coles and Coles 1998). On the dryland surrounding both the Severn Estuary and the Somerset Levels the main clearance takes place not during the Neolithic but during the Bronze Age. It is during the Middle Bronze Age and Iron Age that there is much more extensive evidence for activity on the Severn Estuary wetlands. This is associated particularly with evidence for seasonal summer grazing of animals on the saltmarsh and bogs and fishing activity (Bell *et al.* 2000).

CONCLUSIONS

There is as yet no clear evidence of Mesolithic coastal sedentism in this study area. Available evidence is consistent with a model of seasonal movement of which the main element was from the coastal wetland, used mainly in winter, up the river valleys to inland and upland areas used mainly during the summer. In reality the patterns of movement, community bifurcation and coalescence are bound to have been much more complex than this simple model. Whittle (1997) has developed this point in the context of his view that a substantial degree of population mobility continued into the Neolithic as Tilley (1994) and Thomas (1999) have also argued. Use of long-lived routes would seem to be the most economical explanation for the coincidence of Mesolithic and Neolithic settlement on sites subsequently selected for Cotswold-Severn tombs (Bell 2003). Seasonal migration routes may also help to explain the concentration of these tombs at the headwaters of the Usk and Wye, the Thames and its tributaries and the Kennet (Figure 3.1c). It is noteworthy, however, that there is little evidence that tomb sites continued to be frequented as stop-over places after tomb construction; both Hazleton and Ascott-under-Wychwood were subject to woodland regeneration. The possibility should be considered that these tombs were on routes used in the Mesolithic and initial Neolithic but by the period of tomb use the routeways they marked were important in terms of ancestral geography (Edmunds 1999), rather than contemporary pastoral mobility.

Currently most writers on the Neolithic favour a model of a long transitional period from hunting and gathering to agriculture during which a high degree of mobility continued (*e.g.* Tilley 1994). Thomas (1999, figure 2.1) envisaged a gradual increase in the use of domesticates between 5000 and 2000 cal BC. Cunliffe (2001, 157) has envisaged some domesticates being adopted in an essentially hunter-gather economy which continued for a millennium or more.

Cooney (2000, 39) has cogently observed that assumptions about the extent of cereal cultivation during the Neolithic are central to the current emphasis on mobility in the British Neolithic. The problem is that we have a very limited database from which to evaluate the extent of crop growing. Where, in other parts of the country, cereals have been found in quantity, or evidence of ploughing located (*e.g.* at South Street, Wiltshire), there has been a tendency to interpret these finds in ritual terms (Thomas 1999). In this study area the four sites that have been the subject of sieving programmes, pre-tomb occupations at Gwernvale and Hazleton, and causewayed enclosures at Crickley and the Peak, have all produced evidence of cereals. The first two also produced significant evidence for the use of wild resources (Moffett *et al.* 1989). Indirect evidence for the processing of plant foods, most likely cereals, comes from querns at Crickley and Hazleton and flints with silica gloss which Darvill (1987) notes are widespread in the Cotswolds, with some examples from the Severn Valley. Some pollen diagrams such as Goldcliff also produce possible evidence of crop growing from the Early Neolithic (but see Dark, forthcoming). The available data, although very limited, does suggest that cereal growing was practised on suitable soils throughout the region from the Early Neolithic but involved small-scale cultivation episodes of short duration.

The small published Neolithic animal bone assemblages mainly consist of domesticates, particularly cattle in the Early Neolithic (Darvill 1987). Bone assemblages from the Cotswold tombs include a few wild taxa in predominantly domestic assemblages (Darvill 1984, table 2). Here, as elsewhere in southern Britain, hunting seems to have made a small contribution to the diet. This is noteworthy given the evidence for a still largely wooded landscape throughout the Neolithic.

During this period the Severn Estuary would have offered a highly diverse environment with a vast biomass of plant and animal resources. From sea to land these were arranged in the following general sequence: mudflat, saltmarsh, reed swamp, fen woodland and encroaching raised bog in certain areas. The pattern was, however, complex, an indented coast with many inlets and islands. Seasonally some resources would have been superabundant in the diverse, unpolluted habitat of the Neolithic: salmon, eels, other fish and migratory birds. The saltmarsh and bog would have attracted concentrations of wild animals as the extensive spreads of deer footprints show. Other animal resources are represented by finds of two naturally enmired aurochsen of Neolithic date at Rumney, 2880–2460 cal BC (CAR-851, 4060±70 BP) and Uskmouth, 3640–3120 cal BC (CAR-1069, 4660±70 BP).

By comparison with this diverse coastal resource base the dryland and upland seems likely to have carried a far smaller biomass of potential food resources, which would have been more diffusely scattered. It is striking and paradoxical, therefore, that in the Neolithic present evidence suggests comparatively limited activity within the wetland (Figure 3.3), and much of that from the wetland edge, as compared to the concentration of activity in dryland and surrounding uplands (Figure 3.2). The limited number of Neolithic finds is also particularly apparent when compared to the abundance of finds from the Middle Bronze Age to the Iron Age (Bell *et al.* 2000) when the grazing and fishing potential of the wetland was extensively exploited, apparently on a seasonal basis from parent settlements established on dryland. The inference that coastal resources did not make a very large dietary contribution in the Neolithic is strongly supported by the terrestrial isotopic signatures of all Neolithic individuals examined so far. The greater concentration of activity in the Somerset Levels suggests that freshwater wetlands were more used. Overall, however, the balance of present evidence does not provide a great deal of support for the prevailing model that hunting, fishing and gathering continued to make a major contribution to the Neolithic diet. On balance the evidence seems to point to more radical changes of diet and economy early in the Neolithic with the main foci of activity on the limestone uplands and in some areas such as south Wales on dryland a little back from the wetland edge.

Evidence has been recorded from both the wetland edge and the uplands for what is probably deliberate burning to create more open conditions. This practice is attested on the coast from 6500 cal BC at Redwick and Goldcliff (Bell *et al.* 2001) and inland at Waun-Fignen-Felen. Available evidence does not support the view that this environmental manipulation can be seen as part of an evolutionary settling down process as a precursor to the adoption of agriculture, indeed there is convincing evidence for Mesolithic burning from the beginning of the Holocene at Star Carr (Mellars and Dark 1998). On present evidence there may not have been a greatly increased amount of clearance at the wetland edge sites, for which we have evidence, between the Mesolithic and Neolithic, especially given that there has generally been closer sampling at, and after, the elm decline, providing greater opportunities for the detection of short-lived clearances.

It may be suggested that each of the chambered tombs and the later stone circles correspond to an area, which, for a time at least, was cleared. This accords with the limited evidence reviewed from this area and with evidence for the usual context of these types of monument elsewhere in southern Britain. The main concentration of these monuments is, however, on the Cotswolds and Mendip where there are also significant numbers of Mesolithic sites, which suggests the possibility of earlier, so far undetected, impact in these areas also. On the limited available evidence clearings appear to have been mostly small-scale and temporary until the emergence of a much more open landscape during the Bronze Age. This is in contrast to the development of open grassland landscapes during the Neolithic in parts of Wessex, particularly around Stonehenge (Allen 1997) and Avebury (Smith 1984; Whittle 1993). It seems probable that a similar situation obtained in the later Neolithic in the Stanton Drew-Priddy area where henges were constructed; in the case of Priddy evidence of grassland setting has been noted.

Given the new isotopic evidence that Neolithic communities did not make significant use of superabundant marine resources, these no longer provide an adequate explanation for the coastal concentration of Neolithic sites in south and south west Wales. This strengthens the phenomenological case of Tilley (1994) that aspects of place other than resources helped to determine those spots on the landscape that were repeatedly revisited. It can be argued, however, that phenomenological approaches have not sufficiently considered the role that the activities of people themselves played in the structuring of space well before the creation of the first monuments. Firing of vegetation and the routes which people took (Bell 2003 and forthcoming) created plant communities distinctive of those areas in which people were most active. Simmons (2001, 53) observes that the smoke from fires, which would have been especially evident in dry spells, may have marked not just attempts to enhance resources but have been '*a symbol of presence and territoriality*'. This may help to explain the increasingly widespread evidence of Mesolithic burning, including areas such as Goldcliff where a small island wood in a vast reedswamp was burnt (Bell *et al.* 2000, 60). Discarded food, excrement (containing seeds) and probably deliberate transplanting would have marked those spots particularly favoured as campsites as it does the areas inhabited by non-agricultural communities in California (Blackburn and Anderson 1993). Such vegetational marks on the landscape seem likely to have been at least as important as rock outcrops of particularly striking colours to which Cummings (2000) has attached particular significance as a factor determining the pattern of Mesolithic settlement in Pembrokeshire. This is not to deny the special significance of particular natural places in the lives and mythology of prehistoric communities, which has been clearly demonstrated by Bradley (2000).

Our models must take sufficient account of the effects of episodic fluctuations in the resource base. Resources would not always have been abundant and people's ability to survive in a harsh and hazardous world would have depended both on social relations and an intimate knowledge of environments and their changing nature over extended timescales. These two aspects would have been closely linked because social relations are responsible for the transmission of environmental knowledge in spatial and temporal dimensions and in the development of hazard buffering strategies to overcome the effects of environmental perturbations.

Pre-monument communities would also have structured space through the routes of their habitual movement (Tilley 1994). People do not have a monopoly in the creation of routes and anybody who walks across saltmarsh, moorland, long grassland or woodland will often find themselves, almost unconsciously, following the routes frequented by animals. The course and longevity of paths through the wildwood must have been determined by this factor and by topographic factors, spots with especially favoured resources and, in the case of human passage, aesthetic and symbolic associations. The existence of routeways of long duration, and particularly perhaps places which were repeatedly cleared at favoured stopping places, or points of route intersection, are the most plausible explanation for the long history of pre-monument activity at those Cotswold Severn tombs which have been the subject of modern scientific excavation at Hazleton, Gwernvale and Ascott-under-Wychwood.

Notwithstanding these strong hints of landscape continuity, the available evidence points to a shift in the focus of settlement away from wetland and towards dryland at the wetland edge and the light soils on the upland of the Cotswolds and Mendip apparently from an early stage in the Neolithic. Many writers have identified seasonal pastoralism as a key aspect of the Early Neolithic economy. The robust musculature of some male skeletons from the Parc-le-Breos, Gower megalithic tomb (Whittle and Wysocki 1998) would support the view that parts of the population may have had a highly active and mobile lifestyle, but that does not necessarily apply to the whole community, or to other communities. Preliminary analysis of skeletons from the Tinkinswood chambered tomb did not produce a similar picture (Whittle and Wysocki 1998, 165). If seasonal pastoralism was extensively practised in this period we have little evidence that it involved the use of the rich saltmarsh and bog resources that were so intensively exploited for this purpose from the Middle Bronze Age.

The Neolithic economy of the Severn Estuary does not seem to have involved a great emphasis on hunting and fishing, although wild plant foods certainly made a significant contribution to the diet. That range of activities must, however, be part of the explanation for the concentration of trackways in the Somerset Levels. Of equal significance to the wetland resources, however, may have been the routes of social communication between areas of dryland that some trackways represent. That role may be symbolised by the ritual deposition in the Sweet Track of axes of distant geographic origin, Alpine Jadeite and chalk flint (Coles and Coles 1986).

It has been suggested that routes of communication may have helped to determine the locations selected for Megalithic tombs. This might be seen in terms of attempts to reconcile social changes at the time when domesticates were introduced with ancestral transhumant practices of mythological significance, whether or not mobile animal husbandry continued into, or after, the period of tomb use. The emphasis here may be on social communication rather than economic migrancy. The implication is that the exchange of knowledge, environmental as well as arcane, genes and raw materials played important roles in helping communities to survive in a world which, this study area indicates, may have been changing more rapidly towards an emphasis on agriculture and sedentism than is suggested by recent syntheses based largely on the Neolithic archaeology of other areas of southern Britain.

CURRENT AND FUTURE RESEARCH AGENDAS

Prehistoric research in this area has been inhibited by the categories we have imposed on the evidence, for example separations between wetland–dryland; natural–cultural; Welsh–English; Mesolithic–Neolithic. Progress demands a more seamless approach in terms of geography and chronological periods.

Figure 3.2 conspicuously lacks the chronological resolution to investigate most aspects of change during the Neolithic. Few Neolithic sites and monuments in this area have radiocarbon dates but Whittle and Wysocki (1998) have demonstrated what important results may be obtained from well focused dating and scientific programmes, even on material from old excavations. Detailed examination of the composition of the many flint scatters would also enable changes of settlement pattern and activities through time to be identified.

The evidence presented in Figures 3.2 and 3.3 is largely the result of chance discoveries over many years. Extensive planned programmes of fieldwalking have been largely limited to parts of the Somerset Levels. Targeted investigation of possible sites on the wetland edge would help to clarify the nature and date of activity in these locations (Brown 2005 and forthcoming). Fieldwalking of areas around Cotswold-Severn tombs provides a way of testing whether some of these areas served as foci of activity over extended periods. The use of lithic raw materials has provided valuable evidence of patterns of mobility during the Mesolithic. Comparison with Neolithic lithic assemblages in terms of raw materials and tool types would provide a way of testing the hypothesis of a continued high level of mobility into the Neolithic. An especially challenging research question is how we test and develop ideas about the role of paths, routes and tracks in the long term structuring of landscapes. Wetland contexts with preserved wooden trackways offer particular advantages in this regard (Bell 2003) providing we can establish an effective link between wetland and dryland communication routes, both fieldwalking and air photography could contribute. Flag Fen/ Fengate, Cambridgeshire is an example where such linkage has been achieved in a Bronze Age context (Prior 1991, figure 83). Clues to communication routes may also be provided by standing stones probably of Neolithic or Bronze Age date, since a number of examples lie close to the wetland/dryland edge on the north side of the estuary *e.g.* at Druidstone, Castleton, Cardiff; Llanfihangle Rogiet; and Broadstone, Stroat, Gloucestershire (Figure 3.2).

Evidence has been identified for the significant alteration of wetland and wetland edge environments by burning in both the Mesolithic and Neolithic. A project funded by the Natural Environment Research Council is investigating the extensive submerged forests and other coastal plant communities exposed in the intertidal zone with the objective of situating human activity in the context of the whole spectrum of disturbance factors which would have affected coastal ecology (Bell *et al.* 2001, 2002, 2003, forthcoming and Brown 2005).

In addition to the intertidal peat exposures with submerged forests, thick peat deposits are found close to the wetland edge and areas of good agricultural potential. Fine resolution pollen analysis of these areas would provide a further opportunity for investigating the nature of human activity in the periods in question and help to establish to what extent crop growing occurred in the Neolithic. As regards how the wetland was being used the abundant footprint evidence offers considerable opportunities for work on the wild fauna of the area and, now that the sedimentary sequences are increasingly well-dated, it would be possible to conduct targeted investigation of, for instance, Neolithic horizons to establish whether husbandry involving domestic animals was taking place in the wetland at this time.

ACKNOWLEDGEMENTS

The late Derek Upton is thanked for sharing his many Severn Estuary discoveries and Heike Neumann for her work on the survey of intertidal sites. I am also most grateful to the many people who have helped with our intertidal research in the Severn since1990. Collaborative research with, and advice from, Astrid Caseldine, Professor J. R. L. Allen and Professor N. Barton is also acknowledged. Martin Locock formerly of Glamorgan-Gwent Archaeological Trust is thanked for permission to include material from his recent survey of lithic sites in southeast Wales that was funded by Cadw. Cadw has also been the main funder of prehistoric research in the Severn Estuary with contributions from the Board of Celtic Studies of the University of Wales, the National Museums and Galleries of Wales, the British Academy and the Natural Environment Research Council. I am grateful to Dr Shaun Buckley who prepared Figure 3.1A and B, and with Dr Heike Neumenn for Figure 3.4, Margaret Matthews kindly prepared Figures 3.2 and 3.3. I am grateful to Prof. N. Barton and an anonymous referee for comments on an earlier draft of this paper.

Chapter 4

The Wootton-Quarr Archaeological Survey, Isle of Wight

R. D. Loader

ABSTRACT

In the 1990s English Heritage funded the Wootton-Quarr survey on the northeast coast of the Isle of Wight. This project combined intertidal fieldwork with survey in the hinterland and offshore. The survey produced evidence of Neolithic activity including scatters of worked and burnt flint, groups of posts and trackways composed of hurdles and brushwood. There was also rich palaeoenvironmental evidence and recumbent trees in the intertidal zone produced a 770-year dendrochronological sequence. Rapid fieldwork suggests that other areas of the Island's coast may be similarly archaeologically rich.

INTRODUCTION

During the 1990s, English Heritage funded a major project that was carried out by the Isle of Wight Council's Archaeological Unit to survey the archaeology of a stretch of coastline on the northeast coast of the Island. The Isle of Wight is located some 4–5 km off the south coast of England and is separated from the mainland by the Solent. The study area was focused on Wootton Creek and extended for 6 km between King's Quay in the west and Ryde in the east (Figure 4.1). Attention was drawn to this area in the late 1980s, when a scatter of Roman pottery was found on the beach at Fishbourne on the eastern side of Wootton Creek. Further site visits also revealed intertidal post alignments and palaeoenvironmental deposits which were becoming exposed through coastal erosion, and as a consequence Sealink, whose ferry terminal was nearby, funded a preliminary survey of the beach. Archaeological material was found to extend further eastwards, and the results of the preliminary work prompted English Heritage to fund a project that combined intertidal survey with a study of the hinterland and the offshore zone of this stretch of coast.

THE SURVEY

The intertidal survey produced unexpectedly rich results. Artefacts dating from the Palaeolithic through to the post medieval period, and including organic materials such as Roman and medieval leather shoes, were recovered from the beach. More than 160

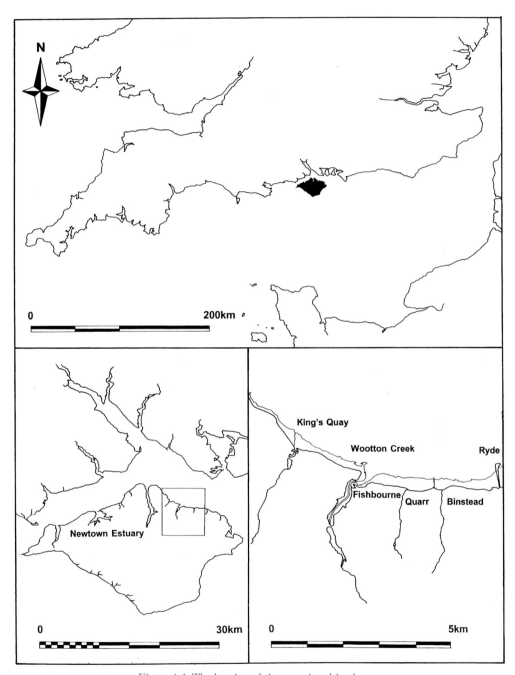

Figure 4.1 The location of sites mentioned in the text

individual features, including scatters of worked and burnt flints, palaeoenvironmental sites, and timber structures such as hurdles, post alignments and smaller settings of posts, were recorded. Palaeochannels at Fishbourne, Quarr and Binstead were traced using a hand auger and were later followed offshore using seismic survey techniques. Peats and sediments were sampled, and analysis of pollen, diatoms and insects was carried out. More than 2900 individual posts were surveyed three dimensionally using total station theodolite, and the height above sediment level, cross section dimensions, inclination and magnetic bearing was recorded. Radiocarbon dating showed the post structures to range in date from the Early Neolithic to the post medieval period. A range of posts was sampled for species identification and examination of wood technology. One hundred and thirteen recumbent trees and 92 root systems and tree stumps were surveyed. Dendrochronological dating of 58 of these trees produced a 770-year sequence. This information was used to reconstruct the environmental history of the area and helped to produce a preliminary sea level curve for the Solent. The results of the survey are to be published shortly (Tomalin *et al.* forthcoming).

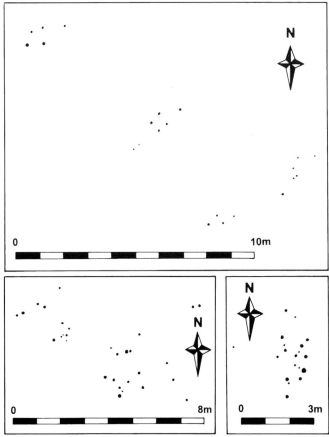

Figure 4.2 Neolithic post groups on Quarr Beach

THE WOOTTON-QUARR COAST IN THE NEOLITHIC PERIOD

During the Early Neolithic period, the north coast of the Island would have been some distance north of its present position. The coastline would have been reticulated by the mouths of streams, including Wootton Creek and the streams at Quarr and Binstead which can now be traced as palaeochannels crossing the foreshore, and which fed the Solent River. These channels would have been flanked by saltmarsh. Some of the earliest wooden structures that have been recorded on the beach are small groups of upright posts located within these palaeochannels (Figure 4.2). Some of these probably represent the V-shaped anchor posts for small basketwork fishtraps similar to putts (Godbold and Turner 1993). Others may be the remains of small jetties or hard standings. The posts that were sampled were in remarkable condition, with bark surviving and stone-cut tool marks clearly visible on the sharpened points (Figure 4.3). Whilst individual tool signatures could be recorded on the later posts that had been cut using metal tools, this unfortunately was not possible on the stone-cut examples.

In the Middle to Late Neolithic, peat began to accumulate and mature oak woodland developed in the study area. Dendrochronological dating of samples taken from the recumbent trees on the beach produced a 770-year tree-ring sequence spanning 3463–2694 cal BC (Hillam 1994 and forthcoming), and suggested that throughout the period the trees were subject to stressful growing conditions. This woodland was gradually inundated as sea level rose.

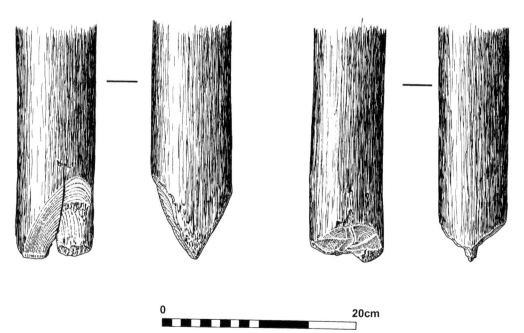

0   20cm

Figure 4.3 The sharpened points of two Neolithic posts. (Illustration by Ivor Westmore)

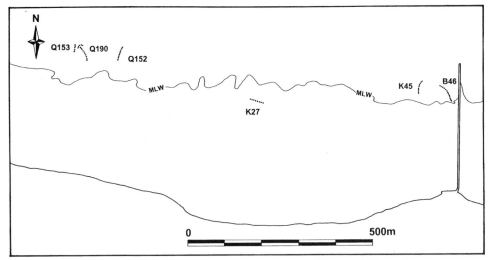

Figure 4.4 Neolithic trackways at low water at Quarr and Binstead

Trackways

The survey revealed five structures which have been interpreted as trackways and which have been radiocarbon dated to the Neolithic period (Figure 4.4). All were found at extreme low water and as a result were rarely accessible. The lowest tides in the Solent generally occur in early spring and autumn and rarely during daylight hours. Consequently photography and theodolite survey were virtually impossible, and there was insufficient time to clean and draw the structures.

A complex of three cross-shore trackways was recorded at extreme low water at Quarr, within a stretch of less than 150m of coast. These were all dated to the first half of the 4th millennium cal BC. The most easterly of these (Q152) was constructed of longitudinal roundwood, split timbers and brushwood, staked by two rows of uprights 1.2–1.5m apart and occasional additional random vertical and angled posts. The trackway was orientated north-south and was traced for 36m. It was of very regular construction with all the longitudinal timbers laid parallel and it appeared that two or three thicker roundwood or split timbers formed the basis of the trackway with the gaps infilled by smaller brushwood and roundwood.

The middle trackway (Q190) was orientated northwest-southeast with a slight change in direction mid-way, and was traced for 55m. This structure was constructed using hurdles supported on frequent transverse timbers and staked by two rows of vertical posts *c.* 2–2.5m apart. The possible remains of a crude crescentic or semi-circular structure at the seaward end were briefly visible at dusk on an exceptionally low tide. The most westerly structure (Q153) was north-south running and was traced for 20m. This was much narrower than the other two structures, and the surviving elements comprised 2 lines of posts less than 1m apart and the remains of longitudinal roundwood.

No chronological differences could be established between the structures, but the fact that they used different methods of construction might suggest that they were not

Figure 4.5 Longshore trackway K27. Note the damaged rod that appears to have broken under the weight of a person or animal

contemporary, and it is possible that they were built in response to a rising sea level, with each being replaced as it became inundated and inaccessible. The purpose of the trackways can only be surmised. Their most likely function was to serve as jetties for pulling boats ashore, or to provide access into the saltmarsh for fishing, fowling or reed collection.

Two other structures which have been radiocarbon dated to the Neolithic period are thought to be trackways. These were constructed some 500 years later than those already discussed, roughly 900m to the east at Binstead. Structure K45, a cross-shore, random, possible double post alignment with the remains of associated hurdling, was traced for 40m. Further to the east, a double alignment of small posts was plotted running northwest-southeast for a distance of almost 60m. No horizontal timbers were noted but it was assumed that the posts had originally held a hurdle or brushwood walkway in place.

An additional hurdle and post structure was observed at the end of the project, and consequently has not been sampled or radiocarbon dated. Unlike the other structures this ran parallel to the shore and crossed an area of soft mud adjacent to the main Quarr palaeochannel. This structure was constructed using hurdles staked by upright posts. One of the rods of the most well preserved hurdle had been snapped and pushed into the sediment below, suggesting that it had broken under the weight of a person or animal walking on it (Figure 4.5).

Wooden structures continued to be erected in the Bronze Age, when a range of parallel sided and oval post settings was constructed at Quarr and Binstead. While it is tempting to interpret these as fish traps because of their current intertidal position, an extensive documentary search has produced no analogies. A complex of hurdle trackways of this period has been recorded at the eastern extent of the survey area. Also in the Bronze Age, the first longshore alignments of large posts were constructed at Binstead and at the mouth of Wootton Creek. These are located at current mean low water and they may represent early coastal revetments.

Lithics

In addition to the numerous prehistoric timber structures that were recorded during the Wootton-Quarr survey, extensive evidence of human activity in the form of flint working sites and scatters of fire-cracked flint was also present. As early as the first part of the twentieth century, the northern coast of the Isle of Wight was noted for the concentration of flint picks and tranchet axes which had been collected from its beaches. Hubert Poole, a local antiquarian, observed 'How far this may be due to organised search in this particular area is difficult to say, but it is an interesting speculation as to whether their distribution may point to the submergence of the old land surface on which the men who made the implements had their hunting grounds' (1929, 657). During the Wootton-Quarr project, 98 picks and tranchet axes were recovered from the beach between Wootton Creek and Binstead, a distance of some 3km. Of these, 80 were flint, 17 were chert and one was as yet unidentified non-local stone. Some were very crude, with minimal flaking, while others were very finely worked (Figures 4.6 and 4.7).

Lithic scatters were also recorded on the Wootton-Quarr coast. These were generally located adjacent to the palaeochannels that crossed the beach and were characteristically found in a hard grey sandy silt that was revealed as the overlying peat eroded. The largest concentration of worked and burnt flint was located on the west side of the Quarr palaeochannel. Flints were first observed on a shingle bank (Q2) and the source was subsequently traced to beneath eroding peat to the north (Q99) (Figure 4.8). This site has produced 2 picks, 3 leaf arrowheads, 65 microliths and 4384 other struck flakes (Figures 4.9 and 4.10). Material was mainly collected from the shingle bank, because it was felt that the *in situ* material should not be retrieved without first being systematically recorded, and there was no scope during the project for such detailed investigation of individual sites, the purpose being to survey the existing archaeology in its entirety rather than to concentrate on individual sites. However, English Heritage has now provided funding for continued beach monitoring and as part of this it is planned to investigate the site using similar methods to those employed at 'The Stumble' in the Crouch Estuary, Essex (Wilkinson and Murphy 1988; 1995) and at the Late Mesolithic site at Goldcliff in the Severn Estuary (Bell *et al.* 2000, 33).

CONCLUSION

The amount of archaeology recorded within such a limited stretch of coastline was remarkable, but there are indications that the Wootton-Quarr area is not unique on the

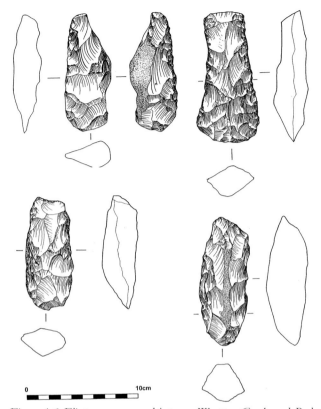

Figure 4.6 Flint axes recovered between Wootton Creek and Ryde

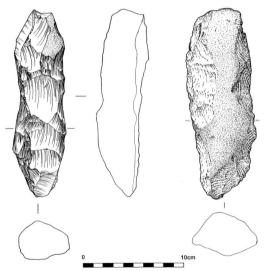

Figure 4.7 Flint and chert axes recovered between Wootton Creek and Ryde

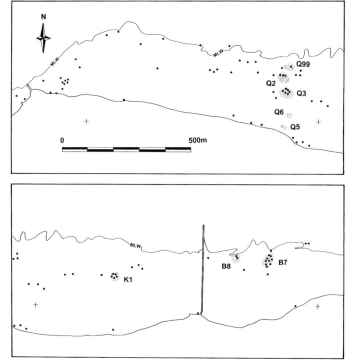

Figure 4.8 Lithic scatters and axe findspots on the Wootton-Quarr coast

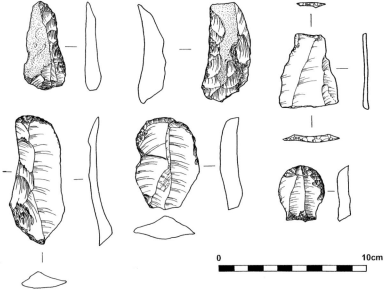

Figure 4.9 Worked flint recovered from sites Q2 and Q99 on Quarr Beach

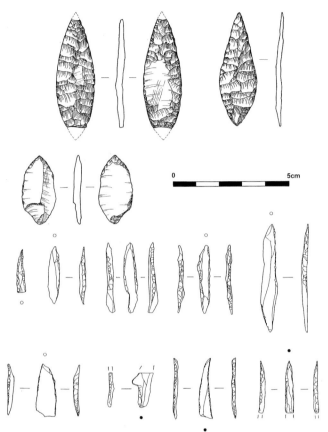

Figure 4.10 Leaf arrowheads and microliths from sites Q2 and Q99 on Quarr Beach

Island's north coast. During the project, a small amount of survey work was also carried out in the western Solent, on the eastern side of the Newtown Estuary (see Figure 4.1), where an assemblage of worked flints had been collected in the early twentieth century (Poole 1936). Two corduroy platforms, one of which produced a Neolithic date, recumbent trees and organic sediments, were recorded during 1993, together with worked flints, hearths, and a Neolithic stone axe of porphyritic rhyolite (identified by David Williams, Southampton University).

In 1998–99, English Heritage funded a rapid Coastal Audit, which examined the archaeology of the Island's coast and estuaries in its entirety (Isle of Wight County Archaeological Unit, 1999). A further visit to the Newtown Estuary revealed more post alignments and hurdle or brushwood structures which had not been visible during the initial survey and which are in need of detailed survey and analysis. Their exposure suggests that this part of the Island's coast is also subject to aggressive coastal erosion. Similar material was also noted to the west of the mouth of Newtown Creek, and other sites visited during the Coastal Audit indicate that there are other intertidal areas that are archaeologically rich. Work carried out at Langstone Harbour suggests that the same is true on the northern shore of the Solent (Allen and Gardiner 2000). Flint and stone axes continue to be found along the north coast of the Island, while hearths and occupation debris are being revealed in the face of the soft eroding cliffs that form the Island's southwest coast. Few of these sites have been adequately recorded.

Chapter 5

The Neolithic of the present day intertidal zone of Langstone Harbour, Hampshire

Michael J. Allen and Julie Gardiner

INTRODUCTION

A detailed archaeological survey of the area of Langstone Harbour was commissioned in 1993 as the result of an initiative by Hampshire County Council's former County Archaeologist (M. Hughes), in association with the Hampshire and Wight Trust for Maritime Archaeology (HWMTA), whose collective aim was to provide development control information for Hampshire's coastal and maritime areas. This paper presents a summary interpretation of the evidence for Neolithic activity within the harbour. The data on which it is based are presented in full in Allen and Gardiner (2000a). Langstone Harbour is an area of considerable archaeological importance and has long been known for the presence of sites and finds dating from at least the later Mesolithic (7th–6th millennium cal BC) to those of recent historic interest. The archaeological potential of the area was amply demonstrated in the 1960s by Bradley and Hooper's (1973) survey of artefacts eroding out of cliff faces onto the intertidal mudflats and by the unsystematic collection of large quantities of flint artefacts by a local amateur, Chris Draper (1958; 1961). The work of these individuals was collectively reviewed by Gardiner (1988). On the strength of its known archaeological potential Langstone was selected as the location for an archaeological survey project employing a multi-disciplinary approach.

The potential of the seabed and intertidal zones for the preservation and recovery of organic archaeological material has long been recognised and also that such areas are often the location of submerged forests that have been of great antiquarian geological interest (*e.g.* Borlase 1738; 1758). Such areas are also known for deep and ancient Holocene sediment sequences (*e.g.* Southampton and Portsmouth harbours; Everard 1954; Godwin and Godwin 1940; Godwin 1945), which offer the potential to provide detailed palynological evidence. Important archaeological resource-bases are to be found in these environments, which not only enhance the record from terrestrial sites by extending the distributions of familiar assemblages, but also compliment it by providing ideal conditions for the preservation of waterlogged organic materials and long pollen and sediment sequences unobtainable from eroded dryland locations (*e.g.* Tomalin *et al.* forthcoming). Thus coastlines with intertidal and estuarine deposits offer great potential for archaeological survival, they may also in the past have provided access to lowland saltmarsh and deeper marine environments and thus been areas which attracted human exploitation.

The multi-disciplinary project involved Wessex Archaeology (archaeological fieldwork and analysis), University of Portsmouth (mapping and survey), University of Southampton (underwater site survey and excavation) and the HWMTA (underwater survey, augering and recording) and commenced in 1993, largely funded by Hampshire County Council. The main fieldwork programme was conducted in three short two-week field seasons (1993–1995), with additional days of fieldwork in 1997, 1999 and 2000. This collaborative research has provided the basis for the interpretation of the changing landscape and activities of human communities within and around the present harbour over the last 10,000 years. Much of this is published elsewhere (Allen and Gardiner 2000a), though here we concentrate on the Neolithic assemblages; the contrast between these assemblages and others at, for instance, The Stumble, Hullbridge, Essex (Wilkinson and Murphy 1995), and the interpretation of the Neolithic landscape and activities.

THE PRESENT DAY ENVIRONMENT

Langstone lies between Portsmouth and Hayling Island on the Solent coast of Hampshire, on the current coastal margins of the Hampshire basin. As a physiographic unit the basin is formed by the chalk dipping in a southward-plunging syncline, and infilled with deep Tertiary deposits (Palaeocene, Eocene and Oligocene) of Bagshot and Bracklesham Beds, plateau gravel, marine alluvium and Eocene deposits, particularly brickearth and raised beach deposits (Figure 5.1B). It is fringed to the north by the chalk of the Hampshire Downs. The chalkland is therefore physically very close to the Langstone intertidal zones and the most southerly outcrop forms the northern margin the harbour. The harbour itself largely comprises gravel overlain with brickearth with alluvium.

Langstone Harbour contains large expanses of intertidal mudflats and shingle banks with sandbanks exposed at low tide and dryer saltmarsh surviving on four main vestigial islands in the northern area, and in the northwest corner on Farlington Marshes. The harbour is drained by one main channel (Langstone) and a lesser channel (Broom), which define the former stream courses. Today, the harbour is a shallow tidal inlet, one of a complex between Portsmouth and Chichester (Figure 5.1), all containing many smaller creeks and characterised by fast running tides. Beneath the present sea level within the Harbour up to 13m of blue-grey Holocene marine silts are recorded over peats (Mottershead 1976) and provide evidence for Holocene marine transgression.

The margins of the Harbour are lowlying with relief ranging from less than +1m to +8 m OD. To the north and west, and on the islands these margins consist of species-rich marshes fronted by substantial intertidal mudflats (Bryant 1967). The islands are susceptible to continual erosion (Perraton 1953) and hence numerous small, unstable and frequently shifting, islets occur. Today the Harbour supports important floral communities, notably on Farlington Marshes (Bryant 1967). The fragile nature of this resource is emphasised not only by the physical erosion of the tidal margins (see, for instance, Perraton 1953; Bradley and Hooper 1973), but also by the decline in some of the floral communities, particularly *Spartina* (Haynes and Coulson 1982; Bird and Ranwell 1964).

Topographically, the harbour itself comprises a number of small but diverse environments making it a physically strenuous and dangerous environment in which to work. As a result of the predominantly intertidal aspect, work was restricted to a few hours

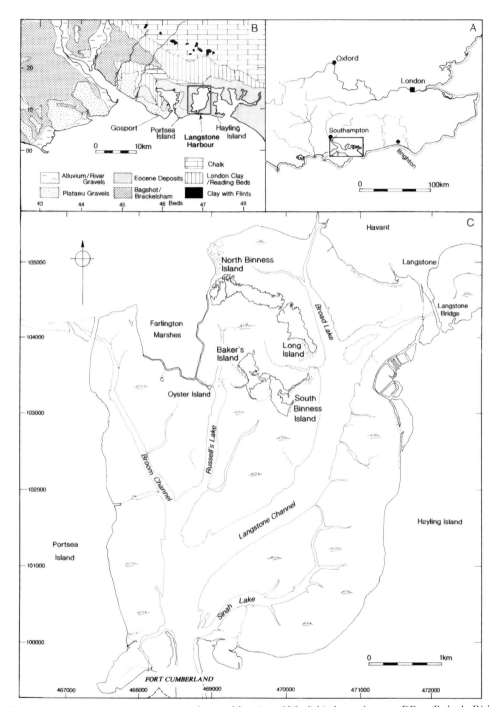

Figure 5.1 Location showing summary geology and location of Neolithic forest elements: BR = Baker's Rithe; RL = Russell's lake (drawn by S. E. James)

around the low tides each day. Langstone is primarily of national importance as an RSPB reserve, and internationally as a Ramsar Site, so that our fieldwork was restricted to about three weeks of the year between the roosting and migration of important bird colonies. In addition to the main water channels and many creeks, the landscape comprises (Figure 5.1C):

- dryland margin with extensive drained marshes at Farlington protected by a seawall;
- the four islands in the harbour separated from the intertidal areas by a low cliff, generally less than 1m high;
- intertidal areas which comprise shingle banks, and relatively firm mudflats through to large expenses of very soft, mobile clays.

AIMS AND METHODS

The principal aims of the Langstone Harbour Archaeological Survey Project were to:

- provide a full database of known archaeological sites within the harbour and map the archaeological resource by period;
- elucidate and interpret the archaeological resources of the present harbour area;
- provide a methodological statement for the future study of this and other intertidal archaeological resources, and
- provide data to enable the formation of a strategy for managing that archaeological resource.

The datasets resulting from the fieldwork would be combined into a full photo-grammetrically derived digital map to underpin the archaeological fieldwork. One of the novel aspects of the collaborative project was the integrated and seamless use of archaeological and geographical methods; the recording, definition and mapping of the archaeological resource, using GPS to facilitate rapid and accurate survey in an inhospitable environment; and the intended use of this data both for standard archaeological interpretations *and* for use as a management database to guide the county archaeologists in decisions of development control. The basis of the integrated seamless approach was that the *same* archaeological and survey techniques should be applied throughout the survey area regardless of modern geographic position; *i.e.* on land, in the intertidal zone, and underwater.

   One aim was to develop a methodology to work in intertidal environments as outlined in Allen *et al.* (1993) and Allen and Gardiner (2000a, 4–8, and 221–231). Our main archaeological aim was to examine the development of the harbour, and included aspects of the wooden harbour architecture, and medieval underwater oyster breeding pens. Therefore the present day harbour as a resource is key to much of the research.

   An initial assessment fieldwork project was conducted over two weeks in August 1993 to assess the feasibility of the methodology, define the nature and extent of the potential archaeological resource and learn how to work in a difficult and intractable terrain. This assessment provided an initial indication of the position (both horizontally and vertically), extent, condition and stratigraphic context of surviving archaeological deposits; their potential for detailed study and mapping; the nature and stratigraphic relationships of the harbour sediments; the relation of archaeological layers to those sediments; and the potential

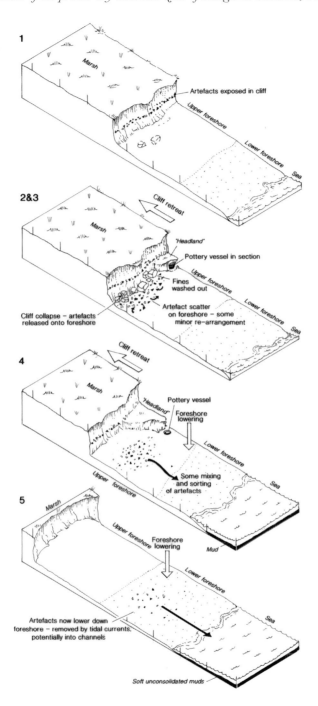

Figure 5.2 Model of stages of recession erosion showing artefact movement, redistribution across the intertidal zone, and ultimate loss in to the marine environment (drawn by S. E. James)

for the recovery of palaeo-environmental evidence. It was combined with an archaeological desktop study and the collation and digitising of existing maps and aerial photographs (Allen *et al.* 1993).

Two 10–15 day periods of systematic, small scale and targeted archaeological fieldwork were conducted in 1994 and 1995. The timing of all fieldwork was restricted because of the requirements of the RSPB, and none of the work would have been possible without the assistance of Andrew Polkey the RSPB warden, and Bob Chapman, of the Hampshire Wildlife Trust.

THE LOCATION OF THE ARTEFACTS

The large artefact scatters recorded by Bradley and Hooper (1973); Draper (1958; 1961) and Gardiner (1988), reside on current exposed surfaces. Recent fieldwork confirmed that many archaeological artefacts are held within low cliffs (less than 1m high) predominately on the southern margins of the four islands in the Harbour (North Binness Island, Long Island, South Binness Island and Baker's Island). However, the flint scatters on the intertidal zone seaward of those cliffs reside on the clay surface; their original sedimentary context having been removed by tidal erosion. Detailed spatial recording of artefacts in relation to microtopography and surface characteristics of the foreshore indicates that the assemblages retain their general spatial integrity, but have been dropped on to the harder, more resistant, clay surface (Figure 5.2). As one progresses down the littoral zone the spatial integrity of the artefact scatters decreases and, ultimately, in deeper water where tidal action is stronger, so do the numbers of artefacts themselves. In reality, around each island and along the harbour edge, a narrow skirt exists in which artefact assemblages are recordable. They are constantly renewed at their landward edge sediment erosion, and constantly removed at their seaward edge by tidal action.

PRECONCEPTIONS

At the start of the project two major preconceptions were held; the first was the long held understanding that the area was a drowned landscape (Dyer 1975) like many harbours of the south coast. As such it was assumed that evidence of submerged prehistoric land surfaces might be present. Such examples have been seen in formerly terrestrial peats discovered in Portsmouth Harbour (Godwin 1945) and Southampton Water (Godwin and Godwin 1940) at depths of up to -9m OD.

Although the area is a harbour today, it is crucial to our understanding of its development and human use to attempt to discern when this inlet formed and what was the nature of this low-lying area in prehistoric and early historic times. The nature of the artefact assemblages may reflect changes in the environment and exploitable resources (*e.g.* fishing, saltworking *etc.*) and herein lies the second assumption. Known Neolithic scatters exist in the harbour (Bradley and Hooper 1973; Gardiner 1988). Major questions to be answered were:

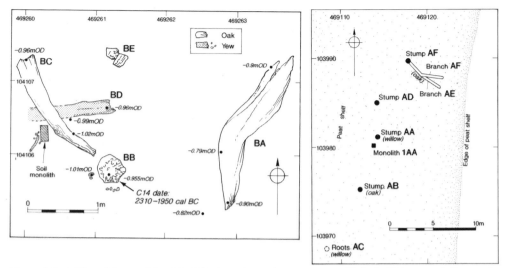

Figure 5.3 a) Plan of the surviving Neolithic branches and tree stumps at Baker's Rithe peat shelf at c. -1m OD (drawn by S. E. James). b) Survey points of the main Neolithic branches and trunks at Russell's Lake peat shelf at c. -0.5m OD (data from Portsmouth University, drawn by S. E. James)

i)   what was the nature and composition of these assemblages and
ii) what activities did they represent, in short were these a result of coastal and marine resource exploitation?

More detail of this could be provided by the palaeo-environmental analysis to define the nature of the physical environment (snails, soils, sediments and pollen), and which aimed to examine the nature of the exploitation of those resources.

EVIDENCE OF THE NEOLITHIC ENVIRONMENT AND ACTIVITY

During the survey, two small relict areas of submerged trees were recorded. One at Russell's Lake, and the second a slightly more substantial area of fallen trees, branches and tree stumps about 175m to the west at Baker's Rithe (Figures 5.1 and 5.3a). Both are located in truly intertidal situations. At the site north of Russell's Lake, wood was dispersed on the edge peat shelf at -0.5m OD over an area of just 25m × 12m. Fallen branches and trucks and *in situ* tree trunks of willow and oak were present (Figure 5.3b), the latter having very close rings suggesting that they might have survived under ecological and physiological stress. At Baker's Rithe a smaller area, of better and more densely preserved tree remains on a peat ledge, was extant over 3.5m × 2m in 1997, but several years earlier it had extended over an area at least 6m × 6m (A. Mack pers comm.). These included oak, yew and alder and were at about -1m OD.

Radiocarbon dates from these two areas of submerged trees indicated that they were both of Neolithic date, but separated by about one millennium (Table 5.1).

Site	OD	Material	Lab Number	Result Number	Result BP	Calibrated date
Baker's Rithe	-1m	oak stump (BB)	R-24993/2	NZA – 10940	3735±60	2300–1950 cal BC
Russell's Lake	-0.5m	oak branch (AEA)	R-24993/1	NZA-10970	4431±70	3360–2910 cal BC

Note: results are calibrated using OxCal 3.10 using the curve of Reimer *et al.* (2004), and all calibrated ranges are expressed at the 95% confidence level (at two standard deviations)

Table 5.1 Radiocarbon dates from submerged trees

Detailed analysis of the waterlogged plant remains from the two peat ledges by Alan Clapham (Clapham 2000) indicated a development from an open fen habitat to one of fen/ carr woodland, with temporary drying-out phases. The woodland comprised oak, yew, willow/poplar, birch, and alder, with an understorey of hawthorn. The ground flora was dominated by species that prefer damp conditions or high watertables, but there was also evidence of open and slow flowing freshwater. There is surprisingly little evidence for any maritime or brackish environment. In fact, only at Russell's Lake, the younger of the two sites, are there a few remains of *Suaeda maritima* (annual sea-blite) indicating that a maritime influence may not have been too far away (although Clapham indicates that the possibility of modern intrusion cannot be ruled out). This might indicate seasonal or extreme flooding events creating some inland brackish lagoons that provided the opportunity for the growth of these occasional more maritime flora.

Low-lying, largely freshwater rivers probably existed in former deeply incised river valleys (Allen and Gardiner 2000a; 2000b) with freshwater pools and alder carr (alnetum). Infilling and alluviation with inorganic fine-grained sediments during the later Mesolithic to earlier Neolithic period presented much shallower, gentle, though still significant, valley profiles (as suggested by the reconstruction in Figure 5.4), which had characterised the area earlier in the postglacial. Although the streams may have been tidal, and the area was a part of the coastal plain, there is no evidence to indicate a strongly maritime nor definitely coastal (*i.e.* shoreline) environment. Direct evidence of trees with notably close rings indicates a stressed environment, possibly caused by this increased local salinity. Extensive peat blankets formed in the wet floodplains in the river valleys. Pollen and waterlogged plant remains indicate that open grassland and alder carr existed in the valleys and adjacent to the rivers but, in all probability, open woodland dominated by lime existed in the main on the drier and higher adjacent land. The fringing chalkland would have supported denser mixed oak, hazel, and lime woodland (Scaife 2000; Clapham 2000).

In the Neolithic then, the Langstone harbour area was a low-lying inland basin drained by freshwater rivers, with fen and fen carr forming in peats with local pools of standing water. The rivers exposed large expanses of river worn gravels derived from the Bracklesham Series. Despite the radiocarbon date of 3350–2910 cal BC (R-24993/1 NZA) and evidence of some burnt flint and traces of charcoal at Russell's Lake, there is only sparse artefactual evidence to accompany this.

There is no clear evidence for activity in the earlier part of the Neolithic. A handful of leaf arrowheads are recorded but represent no more than a few isolated losses over possibly many hundreds of years. Earlier publications (*e.g.* Bradley and Hooper 1973) recorded

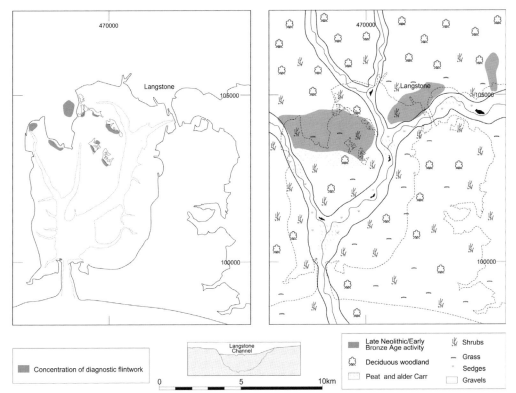

Figure 5.4 Reconstruction of the Langstone Harbour area in the Late Neolithic-Early Bronze Age (drawn by S. E. James)

much of the material from Langstone as being of Neolithic date but, although implements attributed to the Late Neolithic–Early Bronze Age have been recovered, much of the assemblage can now be seen to be later in date. Because of the mixed nature of the assemblages it is very difficult to quantify the amount of Late Neolithic-Early Bronze Age flintwork present in the survey collection which amounted to over 4000 struck flints. Over 90% of the total assemblage comprises cores, core fragments and debitage of which a proportion, albeit probably a fairly small proportion, is almost certainly of this period but which is not sufficiently diagnostic to be separated out for discussion. Table 5.2 lists the entire flint tool assemblage recorded in the survey, excluding scrapers which dominate the assemblage (76%) but which also cannot be separated into chronological groups. A number of diagnostically Neolithic implements have been recovered and, at face value, there seems to be a considerable range of forms. However, it is significant that these all belong to a limited number of functionally related groups with very few examples of each. In terms of the Neolithic element, arrowheads are the most numerous class of artefact other than scrapers, accompanied by a few knives, piercers, fabricators and axe fragments. In view of the nature of the locally available raw material it is likely that the larger core tools (axe fragments) and at least one of the arrowheads recovered during the survey were brought

Location	A	B	C	D	E	F	G	H	I	J	K	L	M	N	O	P	Q	R	S	T	Total
	Core tools						Arrowheads					Flake tools									Total
North Binness S shore west	1									1		1			1				1	3	8
North Binness S shore East														1		1				1	3
Long Island SW shore					1		2	1	1	3		1	1	1		1			1	5	18
South Binness	1						1	1					1			1	1		2	1	9
Bakers Island west	1			1		1						1								1	5
Bakers Island East	4	1	1	2	1+		2				1	2	1	1				2	3	17	38
NE corner of harbour																				1	1
Oyster Island	1																			1	2
	8	1	1	3	2	1	5	2	1	4	1	5	3	3	1	3	1	2	7	30	84

A = tranchet adze/sharpening flake; B = pick; C = tranchet tool; D = hammer; E = axe fragment * = polished; F = ?miniature axe;
G = leaf arrowhead; H = laurel leaf; I = oblique arrowhead; J = transverse arrowhead; K = barbed and tanged;
L = piercer; M = denticulate; N = fabricator/slug; O = tanged piece; P = plano-convex knife; Q = flake knife;
R = serrated flake/blade; S = bifacially retouched; T = edge retouched

Table 5.2 The tool assemblage excluding scrapers

into the area as artefacts; the remainder being made on the spot for immediate use and discard.

Overall, a similar range of artefacts was present in the material previously recovered by Bradley and Hooper and held by Portsmouth Museum, where it was re-examined for the survey. Notable additions are three fragments of polished axe, several other core tools and a slightly different range of flake tools, though in terms of probable function these are, again, all related types (Gardiner 1987). It is interesting to note that the majority of core tools recovered by Bradley and Hooper from the northern islands are of typical Late Neolithic–Early Bronze Age types while the majority of core tools recovered during the survey (twelve out of fourteen) came from the southern islands and two-thirds of those are of Mesolithic date. Detailed examination of the assemblages (Allen and Gardiner 2000a) suggested that there had formerly been a concentration of Neolithic material on the southern sides of the two northernmost islands which is no longer in such obvious evidence having, presumably, been lost to erosion in the intervening years. However, sufficient survives for us to be able to agree with the assessment by Bradley and Hooper (1973) that this is an essentially non-domestic assemblage, possibly representing seasonal, short-term grazing and associated activities. The flint gravel itself was one of the main resources exploited. No contemporaneous pottery is recorded.

The lack of large scatters of pottery and of animal bones like those excavated at the Stumbles, Hullbridge (Wilkinson and Murphy 1995) is notable in Langstone. In contrast to the Stumbles, for instance, we can envisage the Langstone area being used for short-term visits for occasional hunting and the exploitation of flint resources; a pattern of exploitation that continued from at least the later Mesolithic (Allen and Gardiner 2000b). Based on the open nature of the area at this time we can also postulate grazing (largely of cattle) even though there is no direct evidence (cf. Gardiner *et al.* 2002, figure 9). Thus Langstone had the capability of contributing to an important part of the Neolithic economy and life style. The area itself was not apparently settled or occupied; it was peripheral but not marginal to the main occupied areas (Figure 5.4). It was exploited through choice, not necessity, and provided specific and important resources for local Neolithic communities. Long term, settled occupation was largely concentrated on the adjacent chalklands where abundant evidence survives in the form of long and oval barrows and causewayed enclosures (The Trundle), and where there is also evidence of widespread use of the Downs shown by the flint scatters (Gardiner 1988; 1996). Recent excavations (*e.g.* Westhampnett) on the coastal plain, previously thought to be largely devoid of monuments and settlement evidence in the Late Neolithic and Early Bronze Age with the exception of ubiquitous distributions of artefacts, have found the presence of more typical domestic and funerary activities of this period. This indicates clearances within the woodland and of more permanent activities and settlement forms. These do not seem to exist in the Langstone area, probably because of its subtly different local environment and altitude.

Although most of the artefact scatters reside on the upper wave-exposed surfaces devoid of contemporaneous deposits, this maritime, wave-cut local environment is extremely hostile to the artefact scatters. The long held belief that Langstone was a drowned landscape, like many harbours of the south coast (Dyer 1975), has been disproved. Apart from the narrow, deeply incised buried former courses of the Broom and Langstone channels which may contain narrow strips of earlier Mesolithic (9000–7000 cal BC) Atlantic and Sub-boreal land surfaces, the main area of Langstone Harbour is largely eroded and eroding. The assumption and hope that there might be extensive areas of submerged prehistoric land surfaces seems to be unfounded.

Physically these 'harbour' areas are considered, today, to be 'marginal'; indeed they represent the physical boundary where present-day land and sea meet. Their low-lying situations, propensity to flooding and groundwater seepage, and soft geology, make them marginal areas for the construction of modern domestic houses; they are not suitable for residential settlement at the start of the 3rd millennium AD without considerable modification. Archaeologically and conceptually they are also often considered to be marginal in the sense that the areas were not of great importance to prehistoric or historic communities; they were superfluous regions that did not provide significant contributions to the economy and lifestyle. Although, today, many of these areas are indeed marginal for settlement, we must be wary of the preconception since, in fact, in many areas, quite the reverse may be true (see Louwe Kooijmans 1993).

The area need not be in constant, nor intensive, use to make it important, if not key, to economy and lifestyle. The uses of the harbour area extend to prehistoric societies who lived outside the locality, and whose necessities and needs were provided for by the area now defined as Langstone Harbour. One of the significant aspects of the Langstone area is its lack of general domestic debris such as pottery and bone. This contrasts with other intertidal survey areas such as Goldcliff (Bell *et al.* 2000) and Hullbridge (Wilkinson and Murphy 1995). Large quantities of domestic refuse and even prehistoric structures were found in the former, and large assemblages of Neolithic pottery, requiring little, or no, excavation were exposed on surfaces in the latter. The preservation and large quantities of artefacts seem to be features of many intertidal zones; Langstone is no exception, but here those artefacts (largely flint scatters) represent predominantly resource procurement rather than use. The absence of Neolithic pottery in Langstone could be considered to be the result of post-depositional factors but it seems implausible that no pottery of this period should survive alone of all the periods represented in the harbour assemblages.

The palaeo-environmental evidence has indicated that a marine flavour to the area did not really develop until later prehistory, and thus many of the activities prior to this were involved with the exploitation of dry-land fauna and flora of low-lying terrestrial habitats. The area potentially provided a hunting ground for herds of animal, raw materials (flints), and later, grazing or herding for domesticates and even, possibly, local small-scale cultivation.

The area was first exploited for its terrestrial resources, then its marine resources (salt, fish, oysters), and now for marine recreation; *i.e.* it is the water itself that now provides the resource-base in human terms. In this respect then, we can see the role of the area shifting its position through time to the requirements of the population – it *has* become progressively more marginal in economic terms throughout prehistory and early-historic times. In historic times it played an important role in the fishing industry but now is largely exploited for recreation – thus we can see renewed importance to the local communities in the post-medieval and modern times. Ironically it is this tranquil marine environment that is largely responsible for destroying the evidence of its past use.

SOME CONCLUSIONS

In Langstone, unlike some other intertidal sites, although evidence of Neolithic activity was recovered (Figure 5.4), this was almost exclusively flint debitage. There was neither pottery nor faunal remains. At Langstone the evidence is not of domestic sites in a lowland terrestrial or coastal margin but of a wilder landscape that was regularly visited for the resources that could be exploited.

In the first instance this was flint for toolmaking, utilising the large spread of river gravels derived from the Bracklesham Series. In addition the wild landscape was probably home to migrating large animals, and provided an ideal season hunting ground as well as summer grazing. Although, therefore, superficially similar to other Neolithic sites in intertidal areas, the similarity only lies in the date of the evidence, and in the fact that all the sites discussed in this volume lie, in what is today, a coastal, and intertidal zone.

Chapter 6

London; the backwater of Neolithic Britain? Archaeological Significance of Middle Holocene river and vegetation change in the London Thames

Keith Wilkinson and Jane Sidell

INTRODUCTION

This paper reviews geoarchaeological, bioarchaeological and archaeological evidence relating to the Neolithic period in London. These data suggest that the main influence on landscape development in the middle Holocene was rising relative sea level. This caused the spread of marsh across the London area from the east, replacing previous floodplain environments. However, there is no evidence for the *direct* impact of rising sea levels in London during the Neolithic, and the first sediments accreting in brackish water date to the Bronze Age. Vegetation throughout the Neolithic period remained largely unchanged except for minor perturbations associated with the elm decline and there is limited evidence for human manipulation of the Holocene climax vegetation. Oak and lime woodland dominated the upland areas, oak and hazel the lowlands, while the alder carr had spread to much of the Thames floodplain by the Late Neolithic. Within these environments there is limited evidence for human activity. This consists only of isolated find spots and occasional features, although large quantities of stone and flint axes are known from dredging of the present Thames channel. Taken together the archaeological, sedimentological and biological data suggest that Neolithic exploitation of the area now occupied by London was minimal. The authors instead suggest that the main use of the Thames was for hunted/collected resources and as a transport artery.

It is probably true to say that archaeological research within central London (Figure 6.1) has been a largely responsive activity within the last 30 years, reacting to the commercial development that has taken place. Construction has primarily focused on the City of London and to a lesser extent Southwark, while somewhat less intensive development has taken place in other areas, for instance Westminster. The result of this geographic bias as far as archaeology is concerned is that investigations have tended to focus on the Roman, medieval and post-medieval periods when the area now occupied by the City was the main foci for settlement. Investigations carried out of prehistoric sites and in particular those of the Neolithic period have been a great deal less common, primarily because building activity has rarely coincided with features of this period. Nevertheless Neolithic activity areas have been found. Some in the Thames floodplain areas located away from the City

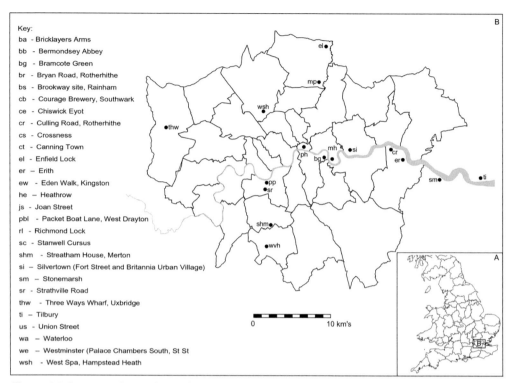

Key:
ba   - Bricklayers Arms
bb   - Bermondsey Abbey
bg   - Bramcote Green
br   - Bryan Road, Rotherhithe
bs   - Brookway site, Rainham
cb   - Courage Brewery, Southwark
ce   - Chiswick Eyot
cr   - Culling Road, Rotherhithe
cs   - Crossness
ct   - Canning Town
el   - Enfield Lock
er   – Erith
ew   - Eden Walk, Kingston
he   – Heathrow
js   - Joan Street
pbl   - Packet Boat Lane, West Drayton
rl   - Richmond Lock
sc   - Stanwell Cursus
shm   - Streatham House, Merton
si   – Silvertown (Fort Street and Britannia Urban Village)
sm   – Stonemarsh
sr   - Strathville Road
thw   - Three Ways Wharf, Uxbridge
ti   – Tilbury
us   - Union Street
wa   – Waterloo
we   – Westminster (Palace Chambers South, St St)
wsh   - West Spa, Hampstead Heath

Figure 6.1 Location of sites discussed in the text within London (Dorney, Eton Wick, and Yeoveney causewayed enclosure and the Mesolithic river channels at Staines are west of the main map)

and which have been developed can be argued to be almost randomly distributed and it is therefore probable that representative patterns of Neolithic activity are revealed by archaeological prospection carried out in advance of construction. Therefore the fact that relatively few sites have been found argues either for a lack of floodplain activity in the Neolithic period and/or the inadequacy of current methods of archaeological prospection for detecting prehistoric sites in such situations. The latter has recently been considered for a number of different geographic areas and depositional environments in the United Kingdom including east London, and is undoubtedly a contributory factor in the lack of sites (Bates and Barham 1995; Howard and Macklin 1999; Wilkinson and Bond 2001). However, as commercial development in central London often requires the construction of deep basements that are dug through floodplain deposits under archaeological supervision, biases of this nature are arguably of lesser importance than elsewhere (*e.g.* Sidell *et al.* 2000). Therefore in this paper evidence for Neolithic activity on the floodplains of central London is considered alongside that of Middle Holocene environments to assess how far landscape 'hostility' played a role in the observed low levels of exploitation.

Radiocarbon dates have been calibrated using OxCal v 3.10, the curve of Reimer *et al.* (2004) and where quoted, date ranges are at two standard deviations and end points rounded out after Mook (1986).

NEOLITHIC ARCHAEOLOGY IN LONDON

A recent overview of the archaeology of Greater London has considered the evidence for all archaeological periods (MoLAS 2000). It is noticeable, that the chapter on the Neolithic (Lewis 2000) discusses significantly fewer activity sites (as opposed to single find spots) than a number of the other chapters, including those on earlier periods. Indeed, this trend has been identified in other, more detailed works considering restricted localities within London, such as a synthesis on the prehistory of Southwark and Lambeth (Sidell *et al.* 2002).

Within central London, Neolithic find spots consist mostly of single, often re-worked, artefacts and objects within an occasional feature, such as the pits and gullies found in the Waterloo area (Sidell *et al.* 2002). No significant evidence for settlement has been found at all in central London and the only features indicative of habitation that are known are recent (largely unpublished) discoveries from the Heathrow area. The Heathrow area also contains a series of Neolithic monuments, which together with the settlements may form component parts of a ritual landscape. These includes the Stanwell cursus, which traverses several miles of the west London landscape, and may be aligned on an earlier Mesolithic landscape judging from pit groups of the latter period found in association (J. Cotton pers. comm.). The other monuments that comprise the 'West London ritual landscape' include causewayed enclosures at Dorney, Eton Wick and Yeoveney Lodge (Lewis 2000). Although these technically lie outside Greater London, this administrative boundary had no impact on activities and perceptions of Neolithic 'Londoners'!

Elsewhere in west London Neolithic evidence is confined to artefacts contained in pits and postholes such as those found at Packet Boat Lane, West Drayton and Eden Walk, Kingston (Serjeantson *et al.* 1991). Limited settlement evidence has also been found from east London, where pits and postholes were found at the Brookway site, Rainham (Newham Museum Service, unpublished data). Although in many ways ephemeral, this type of data has not been recovered from central London. Here evidence tends to consist of occasional groups of finds such as the small amount of burnt and struck flint from the Courage Brewery site in Southwark (Merriman 1992). Occasional structural finds have been made from East London including a Late Neolithic trackway at Fort Street, Silvertown, (Crockett *et al.* 2002) and a possible second example at Bramcote Green, Bermondsey (Thomas and Rackham 1996).

Despite the lack of finds it is possible that direct evidence for settlement exists within central London, but has yet to be recovered. Indeed the same appears to be true of the later prehistoric period generally; a significant amount of late prehistoric material has been recovered from sites such as Bermondsey Abbey, however, all is from re-deposited contexts (Sidell *et al.* 2002). A ready comparison can thus be made in terms of quantity and indeed to some extent location, of finds, between the Neolithic and Bronze Age of London. Despite the fact that only limited Bronze Age settlement has been located, the quantity of archaeological evidence, as measured by numbers of features and artefacts is significantly greater than that of the Neolithic period. While evidence of Neolithic activity is restricted to findspots clustered in the Thames floodplain such as at Silvertown or Waterloo, or on marginal ground such as the area bordering a feature that can be termed 'Palaeolake Bermondsey' (*e.g.* Bricklayers Arms, Bermondsey Jones 1988, Merriman 1991), finds from the Bronze Age are more generally distributed. These data can be interpreted as suggesting significantly lower levels of Neolithic activity, as compared to that in the Bronze Age.

Even on what was probably the optimum location for settlements, the higher terraces to the south and north of the Thames, very little evidence has been recovered for Neolithic habitation. Even allowing for subsequent erosion of these agriculturally fertile areas, this must suggest that even here populations were low.

Late Pleistocene and Early Holocene evolution of the London Thames

In order to understand the London Thames of the Neolithic period it is first important to examine the history of river behaviour following climatic amelioration at the end of the Devensian Late glacial. The Late Devensian in London is associated with the deposition of the Shepperton Gravel following an episode of river downcutting associated with the Dimlington stadial (*c.* 24–18,000 cal BP) (Gibbard 1985; 1994). The Shepperton gravel is thought to have accreted in a braided river environment between 18,000–11,500 cal BP (Gibbard 1985; 1994). Such systems are today characteristic of sub-arctic areas and consist of wide floodplains occupied by numerous intercutting channels. Recent evidence from central London suggests that channel abandonment of much of this multi-channel system occurred during the Loch Lomond stadial (13,000–11,500 cal BP) and that by the

OI STAGE	EPOCH	STAGE	PERIOD	FLANDRIAN CHRONOZONES	GODWIN ZONES	CULTURAL PERIODS	CALENDAR YEARS BC/AD	CALENDAR YEARS BP	^{14}C YEARS BP
One	Holocene	Flandrian	sub-Atlantic	Fl III	VIIc	Post-medieval			
						medieval			
						Saxon & Danish	AD 1000	1000	1000
						Roman		2000	2000
						Iron Age	0		
						Bronze Age	1000 BC	3000	3000
			sub-Boreal		VIIb		2000	4000	4000
						Neolithic	3000	5000	
							4000	6000	5000
			Atlantic	Fl II	VIIa		5000	7000	6000
							6000	8000	7000
			Boreal	Fl Ic	VIc	Mesolithic			
					VIb		7000	9000	8000
				?	VIa		8000	10,000	9000
				Fl Ib	V				
			pre-Boreal	Fl Ia	IV		9000	11,000	10,000
Two	Pleistocene	Devensian	Loch Lomond stadial (Younger Dryas)		III		10,000	12,000	11,000
			Windermere interstadial (Allerød)		II	Upper Palaeolithic	11,000	13,000	
			Dimlington stadial (Older Dryas)		I		12,000	14,000	12,000

Table 6.1 Correlation of chronological terminology and timescales (after Sidell et al.*, 2000)*

Pleistocene-Holocene transition the Thames in central London was adopting an anastomosing bedform (Sidell *et al.* 2000). Bedform changes of this nature resulting from climatic amelioration and dating from the Weichsalian (Devensian) Late glacial have also been recognised in a number of the larger European rivers including the Meuse (Tebbens *et al.* 1999) and Vistula (Starkel 1994), suggesting that the Thames was typical in its response.

Despite the huge variety of sediments deposited by the London Thames during the Holocene, the most recent of British classification systems (Bowen 1999), groups all as part of the 'Tilbury Member' (Gibbard 1994; 1999), named from Devoy's (1979) site of The Worlds End, Tilbury, Essex. Evidence for the Early Holocene Thames is extremely limited – and not just in central London. However, based on data from Staines (Preece and Robinson 1982) it would appear that the anastomosing river of the Early Holocene had gradually evolved into a meandering system by the Late Boreal/Early Atlantic period (*i.e.* 8500–7500 cal BP) (Table 6.1) (Wilkinson *et al.* 2000). Riverine deposits of Early Mesolithic date predominantly relate to continued filling episodes of abandoned Late glacial braided channels, as for example the organic muds and sands dating to *c.* 10,500 cal BP found at Silvertown (Wilkinson *et al.* 2000). Further evidence comes from tributary valleys where organic channels fills dating to the sub-Boreal-Boreal transition (*c.* 10,500 cal BP) and similar to that of Silvertown have been found on the river Wandle in Wandsworth and Merton (Wilkinson *et al.* 2000) and the river Lea in Enfield (Chambers *et al.* 1996). However, of greater archaeological significance are overbank floodplain deposits containing *in situ* Early Mesolithic flint scatters, which have been found from the river Colne in Uxbridge (Lewis 1991; Lewis *et al.* 1992). The latter demonstrates not only that human activity took place on the floodplain, but also that fine grained overbank deposits characteristic of both meandering and anastomosing rivers were accreting by the Early Boreal. Palynological evidence from the organic channel fills at these sites suggests that the grass- and sedge-dominated flora of the sub-Boreal was rapidly replaced by pine woodland by 10,500 cal BP. By 7250 cal BC deciduous trees had in turn replaced pine; oak and hazel inhabiting the floodplain and lime and oak the adjacent uplands (Figure 6.2) (Wilkinson *et al.* in press).

The later Mesolithic appears to have been a period of great stability and both the Thames and its tributaries seem to have been confined within existing channels. These seem to have followed very similar courses to those of the present, while soils developed adjacent to the rivers and were held in place by the dense forest of deciduous trees described above (Wilkinson *et al.* in press). As a result of bank and soil stability there was little accretion on the floodplain and hence no overbank fine-grained sediments are known from this period in central London. Indeed the only deposits that have been found to date from this period in London formed within the river channels in which cross and horizontally bedded sands have been found. The morphological properties of these sands are indicative of moderate flow energies in a relatively shallow entirely fresh water river. For example coarse sands, interbedded with organic muds have been dated to around 5500 cal BC at Richmond Lock, where an accompanying molluscan assemblage suggests slow flow in a channel rich in aquatic vegetation (Cowie and Wilkinson in prep.). Thick sequences of sand channel fills have also been found at Staines dating between approximately 7350 cal BC and 5500 cal BC with a mollusc fauna broadly similar to that at Richmond (Preece and Robinson 1982). On the opposite side of London at Erith sands of similar properties have been found associated with a Late Mesolithic flint assemblage,

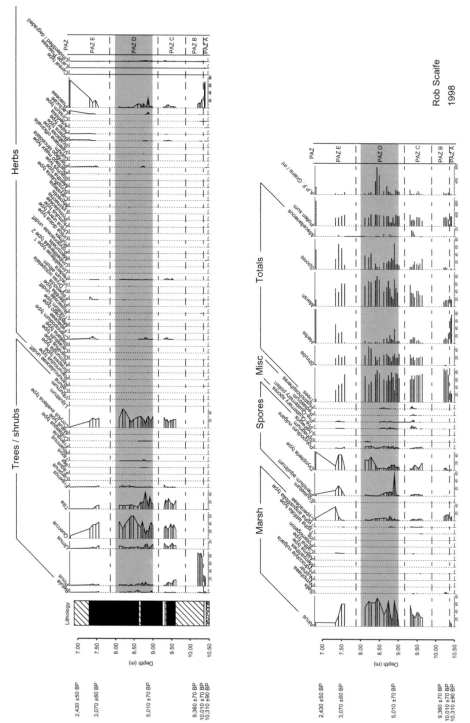

Figure 6.2 Pollen diagram of Late Devensian glacial to late Holocene vegetation change in Silvertown (modified from Wilkinson et al., 2000). Grey shading highlights the Neolithic period

and overlain by a fresh water peat dating from around 4550 cal BC (Bennell 1998; Sidell *et al.* 1997; Taylor 1996). Deposits of sand in excess of 1.5m in thickness are also known from below Neolithic strata at Palace Chambers South, Westminster (Sidell *et al.* 2000). Thinner sand deposits have also been recorded at Silvertown pre-dating a peat which began forming at approximately 3950 cal BC (Wilkinson *et al.* 2000), while at Culling Road, Rotherhithe a 3.5m sequence of parallel and cross laminated sands was found beneath deposits containing Late Neolithic Peterborough Ware. This sequence would appear to have formed as a point bar on the inner bend of a meander and given the easterly location of the site and hence early exposure to relative sea level rise, must date from the Early Holocene (Sidell *et al.* 2000). However, sands do not seem to have been deposited in the tributary valleys and here warm, humid climates and low sediment supply led to the formation of tufas in those streams with catchments in the chalk. Tufas of this type have been investigated from the river Lea at Enfield (Chambers *et al.* 1996) and the Wandle in Wandsworth, although dating of the deposits has only been possible by molluscan biostratigraphy. To summarise this evidence, the Thames at the end of the Mesolithic would appear to have been a broad, shallow and moderately fast flowing river running on a course similar to that of present. It was bordered by areas covered by deciduous forest, rarely subject to flooding, and fed by shallow, slow moving and carbonate-rich waters by its south and north bank tributaries.

Middle Holocene relative sea level rise

Until the very Late Mesolithic the previous comments are generally applicable to Greater London as a whole. However, from *c.* 5050 cal BC rising relative sea levels led to changes in depositional environments of East London (Figure 6.3). The relative sea level (RSL)

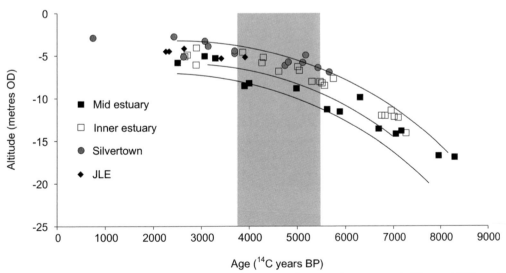

Figure 6.3 Sea level index points for Tilbury (mid estuary), Crossness (inner estuary) (Devoy, 1979), and central London after Long (1995) and Sidell et al. *(2000). Grey shading highlights the Neolithic period*

EVENT	COMMENCEMENT	CESSATION
Thames V	c. 1600 Cal yr. BP (-0.75- +0.44m OD)	no data
Tilbury V		
Thames IV	2750 Cal yr. BP (-1.8-0.8m OD)	no data (-0.9- +0.4m OD)
Tilbury IV		
Thames III	4250 Cal yr. BP (-6.7- 1.9m OD)	2900 Cal yr. BP (-2.0 - 1.0m OD)
Tilbury III		
Thames II	7550 cal BP (-12.3- 6.8m OD)	5700 Cal yr. BP (-6.9- 3.0m OD)
Tilbury II		
Thames I	9200 Cal yr. BP (-25.5- 13.2m OD)	7800 cal BP (-12.5 - 8.0m OD)
Tilbury I	11500 Cal yr. BP	

Table 6.2 Beds, altitude and chronology of the Tilbury member (sensu Gibbard, 1994; Gibbard, 1999) after Devoy, (1979; 1980). Limits of Tilbury stages are defined by Thames event data

history of the Thames estuary has long been the subject of study, but, significantly, the most important published work remains that of Devoy (1979; 1980). Although Devoy's model of RSL change was developed for the area around Tilbury, Essex, it has nevertheless often been applied to the central London Thames in the absence of other models, often simply on the basis of relative altitude (Merriman 1992; Rackham 1994; Tyers 1988). It is now understood that sedimentary sequences found to the west of Tilbury are of a subtly different character to those on which Devoy constructed his curve. Suggestions as to why this may have come about include differential crustal warping and compaction, but recently Rackham (1994), Haggart (1995), Long (1995) and Wilkinson *et al.* (2000) have taken issue with such hypotheses, suggesting that the differences are entirely the product of expected upstream facies change.

An examination of the Tilbury model (Table 6.2) shows that the very beginning of the Neolithic was marked by comparatively high sea levels of up to -3m OD at Thamesmead (Thames II), but the majority of the Neolithic period falls within a phase of estuary contraction (Tilbury III) when the total estuary width around Thamesmead is thought to have reduced from *c.* 4500m to *c.* 650m (Devoy 1979; Long *et al.* 2000). The -3m OD depth for Tilbury II is of importance because in the majority of central London sequences, Pleistocene deposits outcrop at greater elevations than this. Therefore the Thames II sea level event had no *direct* impact on central London, although high RSL during this episode caused marine marginal depositional environments to prograde westwards. A subsequent decrease in the rate of sea level rise after 3750 cal BC (Long 1995) led to the development of peat deposits across much of the Thames floodplain. These formed almost continuously until about 2300 cal BC in Devoy's Tilbury study area, whereupon they were covered by further estuarine silts and clays resulting from a further period of high RSL (Thames III). However, to the west of Tilbury peat continued to form until around 450 cal BC (*i.e.* the Iron Age) – some 1800 years later (Thomas and Rackham 1996; Sidell *et al.* 2000; Wilkinson *et al.* 2000). In other words there is a lateral variability in deposition from the Late Neolithic that is not covered by the Tilbury model, or rather not taken into account by those archaeologists who have thus far applied Devoy's (1979) data to central London. Rather than simply using this model for central London the authors would suggest that it is essential in new investigations to rigorously employ lithological and high-resolution multi-proxy biostratigraphic evidence to develop independent models for this complex area.

Evidence for the Neolithic river and associated environments

The river Thames of the Early Neolithic and the vegetation that surrounded it was undoubtedly of a similar character to that described for the Late Mesolithic above. Nevertheless recent investigations in central London demonstrate that the Neolithic period heralded profound changes in both depositional environment and forest composition consequent of both RSL rise and human action. Undoubtedly the most important examination of mid to Late Holocene sequences in central London was carried out in advance of the Jubilee Line Extension (JLE) between 1991 and 1998 (Drummond-Murray *et al.* 1998). A total of thirteen stratigraphic sequences were examined along an approximate east-west transect (Figure 6.1) using both biostratigraphic (*e.g.* pollen, diatoms and molluscs) and sedimentological techniques (Sidell *et al.* 2000). The radiocarbon determinations that were used to provide a chronology for the sequences were specifically on bed contacts, seven of the fourteen dates falling within the Neolithic. Given that the contacts represent alteration to the depositional environment, the implication is that Neolithic saw particularly significant landscape change in London.

Data from the JLE and several other recent projects indicate that a variety of facies (*sensu* Reading 1986) are associated with the Thames of central London during the *c.* 2500 years of the Neolithic (Figure 6.4). Sites containing peat strata of Neolithic date have been found from Southwark and Rotherhithe eastwards on the south bank and from Canning Town eastwards on the north. The basal dates for the central London peats vary as would be expected given the prograding model of coastal advance as a result of the rise in RSL described above. At Silvertown on the north bank peat growth occurs from around 4550 cal BC (Wilkinson *et al.* 2000), while on the south bank peat develops at Bryan Road in Rotherhithe from 3850 cal BC (Sidell *et al.* 1995) and at Southwark by 3050 cal BC (Sidell *et al.* 2000). Palynological investigation of the peat strata (*e.g.* at Silvertown – Figure 6.2) indicates that the peats formed adjacent to the river in a fresh water carr, where alder dominated alongside willow and even occasional yew, in an environment for which there is no known modern English analogue. On the margins of the floodplain the Late Mesolithic climax forest of oak and hazel in wetter areas and oak and lime in the drier, persisted. However, data from two adjacent Southwark peat sequences, Joan Street and Union Street, demonstrate that the Neolithic forest actually consisted of a mosaic of different woodland environments resulting from local fluctuations in topography (Sidell *et al.* 2000). Alder carr environments do not appear to have migrated to Westminster until *c.* 1550 cal BP, *i.e.* the Middle Bronze Age. Unfortunately, owing to the almost complete absence of prehistoric deposits in the City it is almost impossible to track the rate of carr development along the north bank.

Prior to the development of the alder carr, sand deposits continued to form within the meandering freshwater system previously outlined. Unfortunately these deposits have proved to be a great deal more difficult to obtain palaeoecological information from when compared to the peats because they are almost invariably unfossiliferous. They are extremely difficult to date except by association with surrounding organic sediments. Nevertheless the available evidence demonstrates that in the Early Neolithic such deposits were accreting along much of the central London Thames (Wilkinson 1994; Sidell *et al.* 2000). Examples of fluvial sand facies from central London where accretion began in the Mesolithic period have already been given, but similar deposits of definite Neolithic date

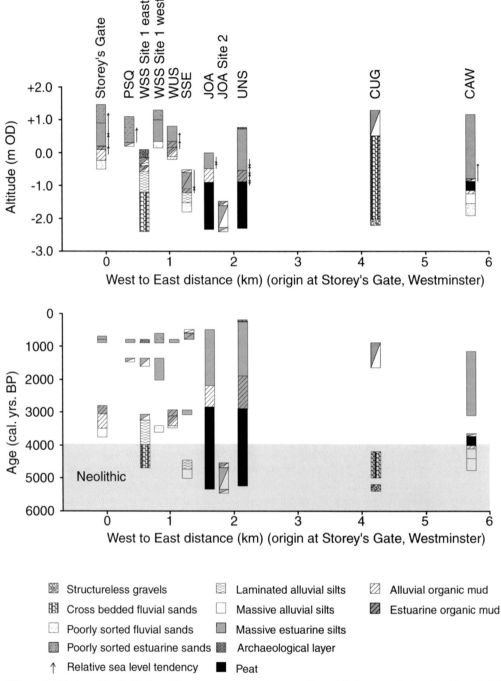

Figure 6.4 Facies of the JLE plotted from west to east against a calibrated ^{14}C *time scale (modified from Sidell* et al., *2000)*

have also recently been investigated from several sites in Westminster (Figure 6.4) (Sidell *et al.* 2000). Beds of fluvial sands greater than 2m thickness have been recorded from around Westminster underground station at St Stephen's East and Palace Chambers South. The nature of cross bedded sedimentary structures and grain size properties in these sands suggest that they formed on channel junction or point bars in a large, low sinuosity, meandering river, with flow velocities of between 0.5 m/s and 0.7m/s (1.8–2.1 kph). This speed is likely to have been combined with a relatively shallow depth, while borehole evidence suggests that the channel was wider than that of the present Thames (Sidell *et al.* 2000). The deposits have been dated more closely than sand sequences elsewhere in London because of the presence of fine organic layers within the sequences. Most significant is the site of Palace Chambers South, where a radiocarbon date from within the sands spans the period 3100–2690 cal BC (Beta 122929, 4300±60BP), demonstrating accretion during the middle Neolithic. A radiocarbon date from deposits above the sand produced a result of 1500–1210 cal BC (Beta 119789, 3110±60BP), suggesting that freshwater fluvial environments may have lasted into the Middle Bronze Age. The first direct impact of increasing relative sea levels in Westminster is based upon estuarine diatoms from organic muds overlying the sands dates from around 1050 cal BC, suggesting that it was only after this that tidal waters directly impacted on the area.

Fine-grained vertical accretion deposits of Neolithic date and which are associated with the meandering river are rare from central London as elsewhere on the Thames. This evidence can arguably be taken for a continuation of the stability of floodplain environments seen in the Mesolithic. Nevertheless such deposits do occur, for example organic muds associated with a freshwater molluscan fauna forming as overbank flood deposits at Chiswick Eyot (Jarzembowski and Jarzembowski 1980; Wilkinson 1998). These strata are associated with a large assemblage of Neolithic flint working debitage (Haughey pers. comm.), suggesting that periodic drier episodes occurred allowing activity of this nature to take place. Overbank deposits of possible Neolithic date have also been recognised from the river Wandle at Wandsworth, where they are accompanied by a molluscan assemblage indicative of woodland conditions. However, in other tributary valleys Neolithic fluvial deposits have not been reported, indeed the period between the Mesolithic and Middle Ages is a hiatus on the river Colne site of Three Ways Wharf, Uxbridge (Lewis *et al.* 1992).

According to the Greater London Sites and Monuments Record most evidence for human activity in the Neolithic associated with the meandering river is in the form of isolated artefact findspots on sand bars (Lewis 2000), although higher concentrations of artefacts and possible evidence for structures have been found at Palace Chambers South, Westminster (Sidell *et al.* 2000). The greatest concentration of Neolithic artefacts relating to the meandering river are, however, from the present river channel, where dredging and foreshore survey has led to the recovery of numerous polished axes and pieces of worked flint (Haughey this volume).

In contrast to other 'wetland' areas such as the Somerset Levels, there is little direct evidence for activity by Neolithic populations within the areas occupied by the encroaching alder carr on the river margin. The sole Neolithic structure recorded from the peats is a trackway dating to around 2850 cal BC from the site of Fort Street, Silvertown (Crockett *et al.* 2002), running from a topographic high (*i.e.* the sand deposits left behind by the former meandering river discussed above (Wilkinson *et al.* 2000), north-south across the marshland. Stray finds of flint artefacts of possible Neolithic date have also been recorded from the peat (Devoy 1980; Spurrell 1889). However, palynological examination of the peats has provided information on the wider impact of people on the environment beyond the floodplain margins. Early Neolithic forest modification is recorded by elm declines recognised at Hampstead Heath (Girling and Grieg 1985; Greig 1989), Stone Marsh (Devoy 1980), Silvertown (Wilkinson *et al.* 2000) and Bryan Road, Rotherhithe (Sidell *et al.* 1995) Radiocarbon chronologies from the latter three sites bracket this near synchronous event (the 'primary elm decline') to the period 3950–3650 cal BC. Although it is now thought that the primary elm decline was ultimately the result of Dutch Elm Disease carried by the elm bark beetle *Scolytus scolytus* (Girling 1988, Girling and Greig 1985), one factor that has been used to explain why the elm decline occurred when it did is Neolithic forest clearance (at Hampstead Heath *S. scolytus* occurs at its greatest frequency 0.2m below the elm decline horizon (Girling and Greig 1985). There is limited evidence for human manipulation of the forest prior to the primary elm decline – although Greig (1992) reports cereal pollen grains from below the elm decline horizon at Hampstead Heath – and it is thought that this event marks the first human use of the London landscape for agriculture, albeit on a limited scale (Wilkinson *et al.* 2000). The Southwark peat sequences of Joan Street and Union Street recorded from the JLE post-date the primary elm decline, and rather it is secondary woodland regeneration following this event that can be seen in the lowest part of the pollen sequence (Sidell *et al.* 2000). The only other evidence for Neolithic deforestation subsequent to the primary elm decline dates from around 3350 cal BC at Union Street where pollen evidence suggests local woodland clearance beyond the carr, accompanied by increases in cereals and herbs (Sidell *et al.* 2000). Nevertheless even here the secondary woodland elements (birch and hazel) continued to expand, eventually extinguishing the open areas. Thus palynological evidence for Neolithic activity on the floodplain margins in London suggests that clearance was short-lived. Based on evidence from high resolution sampling elsewhere in Britain this clearance lasted for at most some few hundreds of years (*e.g.* Peglar *et al.* 1989; Smith and Pilcher 1973). More permanent forest clearance for agricultural purposes has been attributed to Bronze Age people on the basis of numerous pollen analyses from London and is almost always associated with a decline in lime pollen (small leaved lime) (Meddens 1996; Thomas and Rackham 1996; Sidell *et al.* 2000). These Bronze Age lime declines are asynchronous, occurring between *c.* 1950 cal BC at Canada Water to *c.* 850 cal BC at Storey's Gate, demonstrating the piecemeal nature of later prehistoric forest clearance (Sidell *et al.* 2000).

DISCUSSION

The data from a number of recent projects indicates that the riverine environment in what is now London rapidly evolved during the Neolithic period largely as the result of a migration of the marine tidal head westwards along the Thames. However, it must be emphasised that there is no *direct* evidence for the impact of tidal waters in central London during any part of the Neolithic period. Rather the freshwater meandering river of the Late Mesolithic continued to flow throughout the Neolithic period, but as a result of higher base levels consequent on relative sea level rise, alder carr developed along its banks, eventually constricting the river within a much narrower channel than it had occupied during earlier parts of the Holocene. The spread of alder carr began from the easternmost margins of London at Tilbury during the Early Neolithic around 4550 cal BC (Devoy 1979) and had reached Southwark in central London by about 3050 cal BC (Sidell *et al.* 2000), an average rate of 6m westwards every year. In contrast to the changes in river behaviour, environments at and beyond the floodplain margins appear to have been stable throughout the Neolithic period; there being little evidence for significant forest clearance. The large body of palynological data that is now available for London indicates that prior to the spread of alder, oak and hazel woodland dominated the Thames floodplain, while oak and lime occurred most frequently in upland areas. Both floodplain margin and 'upland' environments comprised stable vegetation and soil, which was only slightly disrupted by the localised forest clearances of Neolithic populations from about 3750 cal BC, while even these had been abandoned by around 3350 cal BC.

Within London there is only very limited evidence for human activity during the Neolithic in all except one respect. As already discussed there are indications of localised, landnam-type clearances (ultimately leading to the primary elm decline) in the Early Neolithic and isolated lithic scatters, perhaps indicative of hunting activity from both the Early and Later Neolithic, but these 'features' can hardly be held out as impressive against those of other areas of Britain. For example there are no 'monuments' of Neolithic date in London east of Heathrow, no evidence for settlement sites and no indications for long-term forest clearance or farming, which only happens in London during the Bronze Age. Yet all of these are known from surrounding regions, and perhaps most significantly from the Upper Thames valley where for the Early Neolithic at least, environments are likely to have been similar. It is of course possible that sites of this nature have not been found as a result of their lack of visibility due to deep burial, or erosion of the strata from this period. However, such conflicting arguments can be countered by the fact that most archaeological prospection undertaken in Greater London investigates deposits down to the Pleistocene substrate, and that while strata of Neolithic date are frequently found, artefacts or features are not. Therefore the existing archaeological and palaeoenvironmental suggest that London was a cultural backwater throughout the Neolithic; a situation of marked contrast to that of the historic period. The reasons for the paucity of human activity during the Neolithic in what is now London can only be speculated upon. Although it counters presently fashionable theoretical frameworks, a possibility is the hostility of the Thames environment of the Middle Holocene for human settlement.

Looking at the Thames 'floodplain' of central London today it is all but impossible to imagine what it would have looked like between 6000 and 4000 years ago. Areas now occupied by office blocks, houses and roads would have been dense forest, 'wetland' carr and river channels. Indeed the river itself was very different; the tightly constrained channel of the modern Thames is a product of reclamation since the Roman period. Despite the absence of direct tidal effects the Thames of the Neolithic would have been a much wider feature than it is at present. Much of the floodplain on which modern London stands would have been uninhabitable, being occupied by channels of the Thames and its tributaries. Based on sedimentological evidence from sands deposited by the Neolithic river, the Thames would, however, have been shallower than the present and would have included seasonally emergent islands formed from bars within its channel (for example at Westminster and Rotherhithe). Indeed the river may even have been fordable during the summer enabling access both to these islands and the opposing bank. Within such an environment the characteristic activity associated with the Early Neolithic, namely farming, can only have taken place without the need for large scale 'engineering' at the extreme margins of the modern floodplain. It is probable that forest clearance associated with the elm decline took place in these areas. The channel and channel-side areas would, nevertheless have been a useful source of collected plant, and hunted animal resources (both mammal and fish). Perhaps in these areas subsistence strategies of the Mesolithic persisted and even produced similar lithic scatters to that of the earlier period (for example on sand 'islands' at Westminster). The absence of such monuments as longbarrows and causewayed enclosures to the east of Heathrow and commonly associated with the Early Neolithic or other areas of southern Britain may have been a factor of the low-lying topography of much of the area. This, together with the dense forests indicated from pollen diagrams, would have prevented long distance visibility of such features. It may also have been a factor causing low levels of population, or perhaps the absence of monuments simply reflects cultural differences from the people to the west.

In the Middle to Late Neolithic even the limited evidence for human activity seen in the earlier period disappears. It is notable that the development of secondary woodland within previous areas of *landnam* clearance coincides with the progradation of alder carr westwards and outwards (*i.e.* north into the Dagenham marshes and south into Greenwich, Rotherhithe and Southwark). As previously discussed, the spread of carr woodland was ultimately a result of relative sea level rise and consequent base level changes. These same processes would have made arable farming in many floodplain areas untenable without extensive drainage (for which there is no archaeological evidence). The spread of carr woodland along river banks would also have led to a change in the wild plant and animal resources available to people and would have also made communication with the river increasingly difficult by the creation of a transitional 'wetland' zone. Both this factor and the generally high river levels would have made the Thames more difficult to cross and also caused the submergence of the previous river islands. The almost complete absence of Late Neolithic trackways (Silvertown is the exception) within the carr woodland suggests that these areas did not have the same value for the contemporary communities as similar environments did elsewhere in Britain, for example the Somerset Levels. Perhaps this was because any such trackways would have had nowhere to go to, in the absence of large sand and 'rock' islands of readily exploitable terrestrial and aquatic resources (with arguably also, ritualistic significance) characteristic of the Somerset Levels. Instead Late Neolithic London appears to have been a place where the only people present were hunters and gatherers on seasonal or episodic expeditions. Nevertheless, as previously stated above one type of Neolithic 'site' does occur in abundance in London, *i.e.* occurrences of polished stone and flint axes. Haughey (this volume) has demonstrated a clustering of such finds from the modern channel of the Thames and its immediate environs. While it is possible to argue that such finds are forerunners of ritual depositions into rivers well attested from the Bronze and Iron Ages, it is also possible that the concentrations are due to intense human activity in those areas. Accepting the latter argument it could be argued that these artefacts were dropped by people moving through this part of the landscape, perhaps as traders moving either by boat or on foot along the relatively forest-free banks and supplying people of the Upper Thames and Wessex. In this scenario London of the Late Neolithic would be seen merely as a transit route rather than an area of agricultural or settlement importance.

CONCLUSIONS

At present London is the most important settlement in the British Isles, dominating political and economic, if not ritual life. However, London's supremacy is a product of the historic period, and in particular the decision of Roman invaders to site a settlement on their lines of communication, in a location with a ready accessible route to the sea and hence the 'civilisation' of the European mainland. By contrast the *foci* of activity in the Neolithic period appears to have been away from modern London, while areas now occupied by that modern conurbation were almost unexploited. Indeed archaeological investigations recently undertaken in the capital demonstrate that activity sites of Neolithic date are rarer than those from most other archaeological periods – with the exception of axes found within the modern channel of the Thames. Similarly biological evidence collected as part of these same archaeological projects suggest that Neolithic people had limited impact on forest environments which had remained largely unchanged since the Early Mesolithic. Even the well-known elm decline of the Early Neolithic seems to have been followed by woodland regeneration. Stratigraphic data from sites such as those on the Jubilee Line Extension offers clues as to why London was not intensively settled. It suggests that large tracts of the lowland areas consisted of uninhabitable marsh, crossed only by occasional creeks. These wetland zones, although superficially similar to those of such heavily exploited areas as the Somerset Levels, were in fact quite different. In the marshland of Neolithic London there were few resource-rich sand 'islands' and thus limited possibility for the development of such concave economic landscapes as postulated for the Somerset Levels (Coles 1978; Coles and Coles 1998). It can therefore be suggested that the unfavourable environments associated with the mid Holocene Thames caused London to remain a cultural backwater throughout the Neolithic, only frequented by hunters and the occasional traveller passing along that river, perhaps to the areas of denser settlement to the west.

ACKNOWLEDGEMENTS

Much of the data used in this paper has been produced as a result of the authors' collaboration with Rob Scaife (University of Southampton) and Nigel Cameron (University College London), without whose contribution our work on prehistoric environments in central London would have been impossible. We would also like to thank colleagues at the Museum of London Archaeology Service, whose investigations provided us with the opportunities to take samples and hence generate models of changing environment. Our thanks also go to Nick Branch for his helpful comments on the paper. Finally we thank Jeannette McLeish, Tracy Wellman and Rob Scaife for their contribution to the figures.

Chapter 7

Searching for the Neolithic while it may be found: research in the inter-tidal zone of the London Thames

Fiona Haughey

INTRODUCTION

The evidence in London for the Neolithic has until recent years been mainly centred on the Thames which slices the metropolis in half. This evidence consisted for the most part of axes, dredged from the riverbed during the previous 150 years (Macdonald 1976, 19).

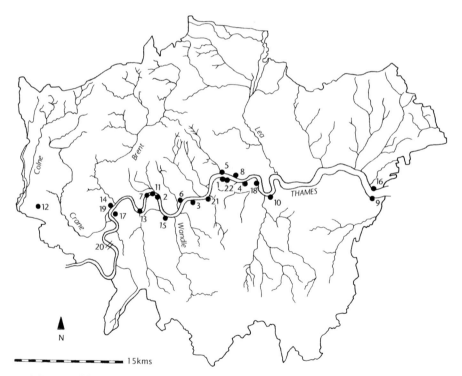

Figure 7.1 Location Map. 1 Bankside, 2 Barn Elms, 3 Battersea, 4 Bermondsey, 5 Blackfriars, 6 Chelsea, 7 Chiswick Eyot, 8 City of London, 9 Erith, 10 Greenwich, 11 Hammersmith, 12 Heathrow, 13 Mortlake, 14 Old England, 15 Putney, 16 Rainham, 17 Richmond, 18 Rotherhithe, 19 Syon Reach, 20 Teddington Lock, 21 Vauxhall, 22 Winchester Wharf

While Wilkinson and Sidell (see this volume) have focussed primarily on the Thames floodplain within Greater London and the work undertaken there principally by commercial archaeological units, this paper will concentrate on the current river channel and the intertidal zone that is exposed twice daily. Consideration will be given to those reaches that are contained within the Greater London boundaries (that is from Teddington Lock in the west and Erith/Rainham in the east) (Figure 7.1). Survey on those areas downstream from this point is still in its early phases and is somewhat sporadic and piecemeal in distribution. The North Kent coast (that is the southern bank of the Thames estuary below the Greater London boundary) and the foreshore on the north bank at Canvey Island and Thurrock are some of those regions the results from which are eagerly awaited. The London Thames intertidal zone has been the focal point archaeologically speaking in one form or another for the past 200 years and it is this focus that will be examined here. A synopsis of previous and current work will be presented and the findings discussed. Implications from these results will be analysed and a number of suggestions as to future work will be examined. Dictates of space mean that only the river finds will be reviewed here but it must be acknowledged that to concentrate exclusively on either those from the land sites or those from the river is to not reveal the whole picture.

EARLIER WORK

Work undertaken on the estuaries of the Severn (Bell *et al.* 2000) and the Humber (Van de Noort 2004) has been acknowledged in a number of publications produced in the past 20 years. However, compared with these and other major British estuaries that have been surveyed over the past few decades, the London Thames is unique in that it is now an urban river, shaped and reshaped over the past two millennia by the settlements that have lived on its banks and tributaries. The constraints of such an environment have placed extra strains on the survival rate of archaeology particularly those predating the foundation of Roman *Londinium*.

Until the mid 1990s, the recovery of artefacts was carried out on an ad hoc or opportunistic basis. The earlier need, for example, for a navigable central channel meant that dredging was undertaken at regular intervals which proved to be both a blessing and curse for the underlying archaeology. A large number of artefacts, which may otherwise have never been uncovered, were retrieved by the dredgermen and sold to collectors and the like with all the inherent complications of provenancing. The range, quality and volume of these objects have been documented elsewhere in number of catalogues (for example Adkins and Jackson 1978; Field 1989; Lawrence 1929; Trump 1962) but no real effort has been made to place them within the context of the river and its floodplain, with the exception of Bradley (1998). A closer examination of the objects themselves and the original museum accession entry often reveals more data than that which makes it onto a computer database. Their full potential has hitherto not been explored as reference is usually made only to the difficulty of pinpointing their findspots (for example Wilkinson and Sidell, this volume, MoLAS 2000) but this is to ignore a large body of valuable information.

Mudlarkers have a long history on the Thames foreshore. Originally a name given to scavengers who searched the mud on the foreshore at low tide for coal dropped into the river from the many vessels in the port of London, it has since been applied more widely to those who search for artefacts (nowadays more frequently with the aid of metal-detectors) often for remuneration. Any finds so recovered are required to be reported to the Museum of London in order to record their findspot but this unfortunately is not always the case.

Another less systematic method of collection has been by those who literally have just picked up objects and reported them to the local museum. An illustration of this can be seen on Chiswick Eyot where a large number of such finds were gathered by a member of the public exercising his dog on the river and now form the Rivett-Carnack collection at the Gunnersbury Park museum. These finds prompted more careful survey in the 1960s on the now defunct downstream end of the Eyot, long since eroded away. A more structured approach has been to organise fieldwalking in (currently) a limited number of locations. One such site was at Vauxhall during the recording of a Time Team programme, where a wide range of prehistoric material was recovered from a fairly small area (Taylor 2001, 21). Other locations include Bermondsey, Chelsea and Bankside. While many of the artefacts are not in a primary context, a significant number have been found *in situ* in clay and peat beds.

The results from all these three methods of collection have now been assessed in the same way as finds that have been recorded on large field survey projects (for example Gates 1975).

Excavation *per se* has been rare on the foreshore. The lack of value placed on these deposits has been part of the cause. Also the inherent difficulty in working within the tight time constraints imposed by the tide has made such work unattractive. Until more recently any encroachments onto the relatively cheap ground of the foreshore, were undertaken without due regard to the underlying deposits. The foreshore, particularly in the City reaches, was as seen as usable land back even as far as the Roman period with the building of four quays out from the river bank in front of Londinium (Brigham *et al.* 1996). This expansion can be seen continuing throughout the medieval period and beyond (for example Milne and Milne 1982). Where archaeology was uncovered (such as the boats found at Blackfriars in the 1960s), often little time could be given to the recording and possible removal (Marsden nd). A major exception to this was a number of excavations undertaken at Old England, Syon Reach, initially by Mortimer Wheeler (1929) and later by Ivor Noel Hume (1956, 43–44) and Roy Canham (1978, 32). Wheeler was searching for a 'lake village' comparable to those found at the time in Switzerland. He found a number of hurdles, which he interpreted as hut bases and walls (Wheeler 1929, 25–27). Hume and Canham similarly found wattle panels at other places along the same stretch of foreshore, which is more suggestive of a number of trackways akin to those found in the Thames floodplain and elsewhere (Meddens 1996; Raftery 1996). The north side of Syon Reach is the only remaining stretch of what might be termed 'natural' bank on the London Thames (Rachael Hill pers. comm.) and the only Special Site of Scientific Interest (SSSI). The water meadows abutting the river form part of the Syon House estate and with the exception of the remains of a jetty (possibly Tudor in date) and an Anglo-Saxon fishtrap, have been left free of the walls and artificial banking found everywhere else.

Recently a small number of developer-funded excavations have taken place in advance of construction of modern buildings, jetties, bridges and pontoons (for example, MoLAS 1998). In one place, part of the river wall itself was removed and rebuilt. In the past three years, a number of instances of the retrieval of human skeletal material have necessitated excavation on a small scale. For the most part, intrusion has been kept to a minimum. Where holes have been dug on the riverbed, the water itself continues to 'excavate' long after the site has been backfilled, resulting in a loss of material, as well as context, and often causes the creation of pockets of soft and dangerous quicksand.

In an effort to quantify what may be found now in context within the inter-tidal zone, 1996 (following a pilot study the previous year), saw the Thames Archaeological Survey (TAS) begin a three-year baseline study of the Thames foreshore, initially from Teddington Lock to Greenwich which, by the close, had extended to the eastern Greater London boundary at Erith and Rainham (Milne *et al.* 1997; Haughey 2003). This had been set-up in part as a response to certain articles written by Nick Merriman, then of the Museum of London and latterly at the Institute of Archaeology, UCL in which he put forward the case for prehistory in central London (Merriman 1987; 1992). Until this, the view expressed by Biddle and Hudson in their publication *The Future of London's Past* in which prehistoric settlement in the London basin as a whole was seen as 'transitory' held most sway amongst the archaeological community (Biddle and Hudson 1973, 12). The artefactual evidence accrued from the dredgermen alone had indicated a hidden wealth of knowledge that needed exploring. TAS was set up to provide a framework for that data. It was a collaborative venture between the Environment Agency, UCL, the Museum of London and English Heritage and with the exception of the foreshore officer, Mike Webber, was undertaken by volunteers from both the Institute of Archaeology and the local archaeology and history societies. At its peak, over 200 people were to be found down on the river, recording structures, features, artefact scatters and environmental data (Haughey 2000, 109).

Since the end of the survey, two of the societies have carried on monitoring their own particular areas and a small number of individuals have continued investigations in others. The river is in a constant state of change with accretion and erosion taking place continually along its entire length. Heavy flooding upstream in the non-tidal Upper Thames region can, and has, caused massive stripping of foreshore deposits further downstream in areas where temporary expansion of the waters is prohibited by the straitjacket of the embankments. Empirical observation has demonstrated the removal of between 200–300mm during the last major event, resulting in the elimination of some features and the expansion of others. If this should occur even at intervals of 5 years, it does not require much imagination to see that these fragile archaeological layers are under threat from something that cannot be controlled. TAS gave a snapshot in time in the late 1990s of what could be found then. A decade later, some parts of the foreshore are unrecognisable when compared with these plans produced earlier.

EVIDENCE FROM THE FORESHORE

Finds from the Neolithic period from the London Thames and its foreshore can be divided into two categories – environmental and artefactual. No structures have been recorded from the intertidal zone thus far but this is not surprising given the effects of the water currents and the dearth of settlement data in the rest of London as well as England as a whole. Other estuaries have produced structural evidence, albeit of a range of periods, but the urban Thames has constraints to which these other locations, such as the Humber and the Severn are not subject. The embanking referred to above, begun under the Romans and only ceasing in the 1960s, has made the river in central London little more than a tidal canal. The vigorous effects of both the fluvial and marine currents have produced an extremely dynamic environment, which is sometimes exacerbated by major flooding events further upstream in the Thames basin. In addition, the wash from passing vessels within the narrow confines of the river channel can have a marked effect on any exposed fragile remains on the riverbed. Hume noted this whilst excavating a wattle hurdle, which, having been revealed and photographed, was destroyed by boat wash before it could be drawn (Hume 1956, 43–44). Given the sheer size of the Thames foreshore and the lack of personnel to undertake the task, it is impossible to monitor it all and thus the potential loss of information is quite large. Syon Reach, once so productive, may be considered archaeologically sterile, outwith the jetty and fishtrap referred to above, having been stripped down to the underlying gravel beds. Conversely and somewhat ironically, now would seem to be the optimum time for recording Neolithic land surfaces in the intertidal zone. Earlier work by Milne *et al.* on the tidal head of the Thames, has suggested that the current range between the lowest and highest astronomical tides is now sufficiently large to expose the Neolithic strata on the inner estuary (the area here under discussion) (Milne *et al.* 1983, 22).

The change the river was undergoing from a freshwater to an estuarine regime during the majority of the Neolithic period and the alteration from an braided system, in channel size, depth and consistency could explain why there is no monumental evidence, to date, on the foreshore (Sidell *et al.* 2000, 109). While at least one causewayed enclosure is known to have suffered inundation at intervals this is not an obviously regular and acceptable seasonal pattern (Pryor and Kinnes 1982, 124). A growing concentration of Neolithic monumental structures lies on the western borders of the Greater London area, in a region bounded by the rivers Thames, Colne and Crane, and Yeading Brook. To the south runs a section of the non-tidal Thames in an area, which even today is notable for its number of lakes both natural and man-made. Excavations at and within the locality of Heathrow airport, which lies in the centre of this defined landscape, have uncovered a causewayed enclosure as well as cursus and henge monuments (for example Robertson-Mackay, 1987).

It is not entirely surprising that the greatest number of features of the Neolithic period recorded during the survey should be environmental in nature. The peat beds laid down along the river channel as the freshwater current slowed in advance of the encroaching tidal head can still be traced on the foreshore (Haughey 1999, 17–18). In a number of places, such as at Syon Reach, all that remains today is residual patches, some of which may have been re-deposited from sites further upstream. Other locations still have a significant depth of peat. At the Winchester Wharf site, for example, which lies adjacent to the south side of London Bridge, it has been shown that the peat which stretches for over 150m is between 1m and 1.20m in depth (Martin Bates pers. comm.). This site has the earliest dates measured thus far for the Neolithic period. A cut timber buried in the peat and at extreme low water has been dated to 3950–3630 cal BC (Beta-147039; 4960±70 BP) and an alder stump found at the point the peat bed emerges from under the current gravel overburden to 3800–3350 cal BC (Beta-148236; 4870±70 BP). Upstream at Chelsea, a less substantial peat bed has dates ranging from 3650–3370 cal BC at the top to 3940–3650 cal BC at the base (OxA-7033; 4770±50 BP, OxA-7034; 4970±45 BP). Both of these sites include submerged mixed species woodland that is gradually being uncovered as the peat overburden is eroded. The largest submerged forest has been noted at Erith where over 1600 trees and root systems lie exposed at low tide. The basal and upper age of the peat in which the trees are rooted is 2530–2190 cal BC and 1000–970 cal BC (Beta-147033; 3910±70 BP and Beta-147031; 2710±60 BP) (Seel 2001; Haughey 2003, 64).

Isolated tree stumps have been noted at almost every location along the Thames often but not exclusively in association with the peat beds. Alder scrub has been recorded at a large number of sites including Richmond, Barn Elms, Vauxhall, Blackfriars, Winchester Wharf and Bermondsey (Haughey 1999). Since the last major erosion event on the river referred to above, it has been noticeable that more trees and scrub have been exposed and at the same time the pre-existing woodland has sometimes been depleted. The majority of these exposures remain as yet undated.

It is possible that some of the timbers in the peat are in fact remains of buried trackways. In addition, where the wood has been eroded out of the peat it is possible to see patterns in the way the timbers were laying prior to erosion. More extensive work recording this patterning is needed on those locations with greater accessibility and less fragile examples, such as that at Putney and Winchester Wharf. The effects of the twin currents on the river removes such tenuous archaeological remains very quickly and the lack of a large work force on the Thames at present probably means that many such examples are disappearing before their potential has been recognised.

There has been a significant quantity of bone recovered from the Thames and its foreshore, both animal and human. While the majority is undated and from secondary contexts, some has been found within more archaeologically valuable locations. Bone (for example, shoulder blades, long bones and jaws) have been found in secure contexts (primarily from the Neolithic peat beds) on a range of sites along the river from Richmond in the west through to Rainham in the east and have included red deer, wild boar and horse. A bone awl was recovered recently from Chelsea. Human material, principally in the form of skulls was collected by the dredgermen. Given the average person's difficulty in identifying the difference between animal and human skeletal material, it is not surprising that the men working the dredgers produced items of bone that were undeniably human when requested to do so by the antiquarian collectors. Very few of these have been dated and only one to date has been assigned to the Neolithic period. This was found at Battersea, is a female *c.* 25 years old and is dated to 3800–3520 cal BC (OxA-1199; 4880±80 BP). During the past two years, an increasing number of human remains have been recovered *in situ* from a range of locations on the river including Chelsea, Rotherhithe, Bermondsey and Vauxhall. None of these so far has been recognised as Neolithic but if this trend continues in tandem with the increasing erosion, it is highly probable that this may soon be the case.

Organic artefacts recovered include those made of antler and horn, which were found in abundance by the dredgermen, principally on sites upstream from Vauxhall, although they are more rare these days. Two recent examples are a pair of red deer antler-beam mattocks found at Mortlake (Cotton and Green 2005, 126–128). So far unique on the

Thames, is the wooden 'beater' that was found in the peat at Chelsea amongst but not necessarily in association with a large number of the animal bone pieces and which has produced a Neolithic date 3630–3350 cal BC (Beta-117088; 4660±50 BP) (Webber 2004) (Figure 7.2).

In the past, pottery in the form of whole vessels as well as sherds from the Neolithic period was not common from the foreshore, particularly when compared with the average dryland site. Only four whole pots (three from Mortlake and one Late Neolithic example from Hammersmith) have been recorded. Until recently Mortlake was also the principal site for sherds with almost all the rest from Hammersmith and Chiswick Eyot. Peterborough and Ebbsfleet ware were dominant with occasional pieces of Abingdon ware. There are a number of possible reasons for this apparent lack of ceramic material, not least is the survival rate in such a dynamic landscape and also the fact that for the most part these were collected by the dredgermen for suitable remuneration from the antiquarians. Whole bowls no doubt commanded a higher price than mere sherds. Recently a number of pieces of Peterborough ware have been gathered from a fairly small area at Bermondsey, below Tower Bridge (Cotton and Green 2005, 131–133). The foreshore was examined at regular intervals over a few months by a number of people but in spite of this only a proportion of the sherds forming a single large pot were recovered (Jon Cotton pers comm.) (Figure 7.3). This amply demonstrates the problems of coping with fast erosion rates on the Thames foreshore. Currently, the recovery sites of the pottery as a whole can be seen to be located in a number of discrete locations but this might be an artificial result of focus by the dredgers or merely survival rates. Fieldwalking (as noted above at Vauxhall) on the river at regular intervals will hopefully aid to balance this potentially skewed record.

The largest number of artefacts from the Neolithic period are made from flint and stone. This is not surprising given the principal method of retrieval via the dredgers. However, an

Figure 7.2 Chelsea 'beater' (by permission of the Museum of London)

examination of the range of implements demonstrates a slight lack of the smaller items and a predominance of axes and the like. In other words, the larger and finer pieces dominate the collection, which may be a problem with the collection policy and not necessarily an indication of a genuine predominance. Much discussion has taken place on the potential ritual deposition of particularly the polished stone axes in the river but this is to take this artefact out of context. An examination of the range of stone and flint tools shows that they tend to be found in company with objects made from a similar material, such as flakes, cores and scrapers (for example, Cotton and Green 2005, 127–136, with particular note of p. 134). While much of the material dates to the Neolithic period in general it is interesting to note the collection of Early Neolithic flint tools which were found on Chiswick Eyot along with later flint and ceramic items. Work on the Humber noted the importance of riverside locations and islands during the Early Neolithic (Van de Noort 2004, 36, 41) and it would seem that this pattern might be also found on the Thames.

DISCUSSION

There is currently a tendency to suggest that the Thames within the Greater London area was not one regularly frequented during the Neolithic, and more particularly in the early part of the period but this seems to be a view that dismisses the evidence that is already available as well as to disallow the possibility of future artefacts and the like, emerging from beneath the eroding surface of the foreshore. With the current tidal range being favourable to exposure of the Neolithic levels, as referred to above, and the increasing

Figure 7.3 Peterborough Ware sherds from Bermondsey

rates of erosion, the expectation of Neolithic material should be much higher than hitherto. Given the physical constraints of the river within its urban surroundings, it seems unlikely that it would be possible to uncover signs of settlement on the floodplain. Indeed, this lack of settlement sites in England is a well-known conundrum of the Neolithic period. The Stonehenge landscape, for example, is not one that has suffered from river inundation such as the Thames nor one that that has a huge urban complex built upon it. This might explain in part the preservation of a large number of monuments and barrows. The landscape within the Greater London area that best reflects the Stonehenge complex is that within the Colne and Thames to the west. The use of the river for transport to and from this special area through the wooded areas which bounded the Thames as well as the marshy areas immediately adjacent to it, would have been vital, if not the only means of 'entry' to the landscape. In addition, it would have been the main method of trade within and through the area as the number of foreign axes recovered from its confines attest (for example, Adkins and Jackson 1978, 10, 13; Cotton and Green 2005, 129) The deposits laid down by the river during its various inundations of the floodplain have created an extremely deep layer of alluvial material which acts as a blanket over all the potential underlying archaeology. An example of this has been found on the A13 excavation for example, where the somewhat elusive Early Neolithic material was recorded at a significant depth (Gifford nd, 38). In addition, the braided river system in evidence for at least part of the Neolithic and the encroaching estuarine conditions add a layer of uncertainty over what may be considered river bed and what may be considered dry land at that time (Sidell *et al.* 2000, 107–109). The submerged forest, now found on the foreshore and lying close to the current river channel, illustrates this difficulty.

The lack of publication of the findings from TAS and work since has been a major obstacle to disseminating the information of what has been found on the Thames foreshore. While there have been a number of useful volumes produced detailing research on the adjacent land sites (for example, Museum of London 2000, Sidell *et al.* 2000, Sidell *et al.* 2002), there has been little from the inter-tidal zone itself. The reports generated by developer-funded excavations and surveys have not reached the public domain (for example, MoLAS 1998). Those that have been available have tended to be either syntheses or descriptions of early work (Cowie and Eastmond 1997; Milne *et al.* 1997; Haughey 1999; 2000; 2003). Latterly, theoretical research and debate has begun to be undertaken (Haughey in press). It is to be hoped that individual sites will be published in the near future with in-depth discussion .

Lack of funding, especially since 1999, has been a major handicap to the work on the river particularly for dating and analysis as well as the aforementioned publications. A significant number of people have given freely of their time and expertise but it would appear that a key archaeological resource is disappearing before our eyes with much of its potential either untapped or unobserved. The speed with which deposits and artefacts are eroding from the riverbed is measurable. It behoves us to not waste its potential.

ACKNOWLEDGEMENT

My thanks to Subhadra Das for drawing Figure 7.1

Chapter 8

Bibliography

Adkins, R. and Jackson, R. (1978) *Neolithic Stone and Flint Axes from the River Thames.* London, British Museum Occasional Paper no.1.

Aldhouse-Green, S. H. R. (2000) Palaeolithic and Mesolithic Wales. In Lynch F., Aldhouse-Green, S. and Davies, J. L. *Prehistoric Wales.* Stroud, Sutton, 1–41.

Aldhouse-Green, S. H. R., Whittle, A. W. R., Allen, J. R. L., Caseldine, A. E., Culver S. J., Day H., Lundqvist J. and Upton D. (1992) Prehistoric human footprints from the Severn Estuary at Uskmouth and Magor Pill, Gwent, Wales. *Archaeologia Cambrensis* 41, 14–55.

Allen, J. R. L. (1987) Late Flandrian shoreline oscillations in the Severn Estuary: the Rumney Formation and its typesite. *Philosophical Transactions of the Royal Society of London* B315, 157–74.

Allen, J. R. L. (1990) Three Neolithic axes from the Severn Estuary. *Transactions of the Bristol and Gloucestershire Archaeological Society* 108, 171–4.

Allen, J. R. L. (1997) Subfossil mammalian tracks (Flandrian) in the Severn Estuary, SW Britain: mechanics of formation, preservation and distribution. *Philosophical Transactions of the Royal Society of London,* B352, 481–518.

Allen, J. R. L. (1998) A prehistoric (Neolithic – Bronze Age) complex on the Severn Estuary Levels, Oldbury-on-Severn, South Glos. *Transactions of the Bristol and Gloucestershire Archaeological Society* 116, 93–115.

Allen, J. R. L. (1999) Geological impacts on coastal wetland landscapes: some general effects of sediment autocompaction in the Holocene of northwest Europe. *The Holocene* 9, 1–12.

Allen, J. R. L. (2001) Late Quaternary stratigraphy in the Gwent Levels (southeast Wales): the subsurface evidence. *Proceedings of the Geologists' Association* 112, 289–315.

Allen, J. R. L. and Bell, M. (1999) A late Holocene tidal palaeochannel, Redwick, Gwent: late Roman activity and a possible early Medieval fish trap. *Archaeology in the Severn Estuary* 10, 53–64.

Allen, J. R. L. and Rae, J. E. (1987) Late Flandrian shoreline oscillations in the Severn Estuary: a geomorphological and stratigraphical reconnaissance. *Philosophical Transactions of the Royal Society of London,* B315, 185–230.

Allen, M. J. (1997) Environment and land-use: the economic development of the communities who built Stonehenge. In Cunliffe B and Renfrew C (eds) *Science and Stonehenge. Proceedings of the British Academy* 92, 115–144.

Allen, M. J. and Gardiner, J. (2000a) *Our Changing Coast: a survey of the intertidal archaeology of Langstone Harbour, Hampshire.* York, Council for British Archaeology Research Report 124.

Allen, M. J. and Gardiner, J. (2000b) The Mesolithic in Langstone Harbour: terrestrial assemblages in a marine environment, in Young, R., (ed.), *Mesolithic Lifeways: current research from Britain and Ireland.* Leicester Archaeology Monograph 7, 209–219.

Allen, M. J., Gardiner, J., Fontana, D. and Pearson, A. (1993) Archaeological assessment of Langstone Harbour, Hampshire. *PAST* 16, 1–3.

Andersen, S. H. (1995) Coastal adaptation and marine exploitation in late Mesolithic Denmark – with special emphasis on the Limfjord region. In Fischer A. (ed.) *Man and Sea in the Mesolithic*. Oxford, Oxbow Books.

Anwyl Prof. (1909) The early settlers of Monmouth. *Archaeologia Cambrensis* 6th series, 1 pt III, 262–82.

ApSimon, A. M., Smart P. L., Macphail R., Scott K. and Taylor H. (1992) King Arthur's Cave, Whitchurch, Herefordshire. *Proceedings of the University of Bristol Spelaeological Society* 19 (2), 183–249.

Ashmore, P. J. (1996) *Neolithic and Bronze Age Scotland*, Edinburgh, Historic Scotland.

Balaam, N. D., Bell M. G., David A. E. U., Levitan B., Macphail R. I., Robinson M. and Scaife R. G. (1987 Prehistoric and Romano-British sites at Westward Ho!, Devon: Archaeological and Palaeo-environmental surveys 1983 and 1984. In N. D. Balaam, B. Levitan and V. Straker (eds) *Studies in palaeoeconomy and environment in south west England*. Oxford, British Archaeological Reports British Series 181, 163–264.

Barclay, G. J. (1997) The Neolithic in K. J. Edwards, and I. B. M. Ralston (eds) *Scotland: Environment and Archaeology, 8000 BC–AD 1000*, 127–149. John Wiley.

Barton, R. N. E. (1994) Second Interim report on the survey and excavations in the Wye Valley, 1994. *Proceedings of the University of Bristol Spelaeological Society,* 20 (1), 63–73.

Barton, R. N. E. (1996) Fourth interim report on the survey and excavations in the Wye Valley, 1996. *Proceedings of the University of Bristol Spelaeological Society* 20(3), 263–273.

Barton, R. N. E., Berridge P. J., Walker M. J. C. and Bevins R. E. (1995) Persistent places in the Mesolithic Landscape: an example from the Black Mountain Uplands of South Wales. *Proceedings of the Prehistoric Society* 61, 81–116.

Bates, M. R. and Barham, A. J. (1995) Holocene alluvial stratigraphic architecture and archaeology in the Lower Thames area. In D. R. Bridgland, P. Allen and B. A. Haggart (eds) *The Quaternary of the lower reaches of the Thames: Field Guide*, 85–98. Durham, Quaternary Research Association.

Bell, M. G. (1987) Recent molluscan studies in the South West. In N. D. Balaam, B. Levitan and V. Straker (eds) *Studies in palaeoeconomy and environment in south west England*. Oxford, British Archaeological Reports British Series 181, 1–8.

Bell, M. G. (1990) *Brean Down excavations 1983–1987*. London, English Heritage Archaeological Report 15.

Bell, M. G. (2000) Intertidal peats and the archaeology of coastal change in the Severn Estuary, Bristol Channel and Pembrokeshire. In K. Pye and J. R. L Allen (eds) *Coastal and Estuarine Environments: sedimentology, geomorphology and geoarchaeology*. London, Geological Society Special Publication 175, 377–392.

Bell M. G. (2001) Environmental archaeology in the Severn Estuary: progress and prospects. In *Estuarine Archaeology: the Severn and beyond, Archaeology in the Severn Estuary* 11, 69–103.

Bell, M. G. (2003) Making one's way in the world: trackways from a wetland and dryland perspective. In Croes, D (ed.) *Wet Site Connections: Conference preprints*. Olympia Washington, USA.

Bell, M. G. (forthcoming) *Prehistoric Coastal Communities: the archaeology of western Britain 6000–3000 Cal BC*. York: CBA Research Report 149.

Bell, M. G., Allen, J. R. L., Nayling, N. and Buckley, S. (2001) Mesolithic to Neolithic coastal environmental change *c.* 6500–3500 cal BC. *Archaeology in the Severn Estuary* 12, 27–53.

Bell, M. G., Allen, J. R. L., Buckley, S., Dark, P., Haslett, S. (2002) Mesolithic to Neolithic Coastal Environmental Change: excavations at Goldcliff East 2002. *Archaeology in the Severn Estuary* 13.

Bell, M., Allen, J. R. L., Buckley, S., Dark, P. and Nayling, N. (2003) Mesolithic to Neolithic coastal environmental change: excavations at Goldcliff East 2003 and research at Redwick. *Archaeology in the Severn Estuary* 14, 1–26.

Bell, M. G., Caseldine, A. and Neumann, H. (2000) *Prehistoric intertidal archaeology in the Welsh Severn Estuary*. York, Council for British Archaeology Research Report 120.

Bennell, M. (1998) *Under the road. Archaeological discoveries at Bronze Age Way, Erith*. Bexley Council, London.

Bennett, K. D. (1989) A provisional map of forest types for the British Isles 5000 years ago. *Journal of Quaternary Science* 4, 141–44.

Bewley, R. H. (1994) Prehistoric and Romano-British Settlement in the Solway Plain Cumbria. Oxford, Oxbow Monograph 36.

Biddle, M. and Hudson, D. (1973) *The future of London's past*. Worcester, Rescue Publication no.4.

Bird, E. C. F. and Ranwell, D. S. (1964) *Spartina* saltmarsh in southern England IV: the physiography of Poole Harbour, Dorset. *Journal of Ecology* 52, 355–366.

Blackburn, T. C. and Anderson K. (1993) *Before the Wilderness*. Menlo Park, California, Balkema Press.

Borlase, W. (1753) Of the great alterations which the islands of Scilly have undergone since the time of the ancients. *Philosophical Transaction of the Royal Society, London* 48, 57–67.

Borlase, W. (1757) An account of some trees discovered underground on the shore at Mount's Bay in Cornwall. *Philosophical Transactions of the Royal Society, London* 50, 51–53.

Borlase, W. (1758) *The Natural History of Cornwall*.

Bowen, D. Q. (1999) *A revised correlation of Quaternary deposits in the British Isles*. Bath, Geological Society special report 23.

Bradley, R. J. (1998) *The passage of arms*. Oxford, Oxbow Books 2nd ed.

Bradley, R. J. (2000) *An Archaeology of Natural Places*. London, Routledge.

Bradley, R. J. and Hooper, B. (1973) Recent discoveries from Portsmouth and Langstone harbours: Mesolithic to Iron Age. *Proceedings of the Hampshire Field Club and Archaeological Society* 30, 17–27.

Brigham, T., Watson, B., Tyers, I. with Bartkowiak, R. (1996) Current archaeological work at Regis House in the City of London (part 1). *London Archaeologist* 8 (2), 31–38.

Britnell, W. T. and Savory H. N. (1984) *Gwernvale and Penywyrlod: two Neolithic long cairns in the Black Mountains of Brecknock*. Cambrian Archaeological Monograph 2.

Bronk Ramsey, C. (2001) Development of the Radiocarbon Program OxCal, *Radiocarbon* 43 (2A) 355–363

Brown, A. (2005) Wetlands and drylands in prehistory: Mesolithic to Bronze Age human activity and impact in the Severn Estuary south west Britain. Unpublished PhD thesis University of Reading.

Brown, A. (forthcoming) Mesolithic to Neolithic human activity and impact at the Severn Estuary wetland edge: studies at Llandevenny, Oldbury, Hills Flats and Woolaston. In Bell, M. forthcoming *Prehistoric Coastal Communities: the archaeology of western Britain 6000–3000 Cal BC*. York: CBA Research Report 149.

Brown, A. G. (1982) Human impact on the former floodplain woodlands of the Severn. In M. Bell and S. Limbrey (eds) *Archaeological Aspects of Woodland Ecology*. Oxford, British Archaeogical Reports International Series 146, 93–104.

Brown, A. G. (1986) Flint and chert small finds from the Somerset Levels. Part 1: the Brue Valley. *Somerset Levels Papers* 12, 12–26.

Brown, A. G. (1987) Holocene floodplain sedimentation and channel response of the Lower River Severn, UK. *Zeitschrift für Geomorphologie* 31, 293–310.

Brown, A. G. (1997) Clearances and Clearings: deforestation in Mesolithic/Neolithic Britain. *Oxford Journal of Archaeology* 16, 133–146.

Bryant, M. (1967) The flora and Langstone Harbour and Farlington Marshes. *Proceedings of the Hampshire Field Club and Archaeological. Society* 24, 5–13.

Burbridge, R. E. (1998) *Study of Environmental changes in the Severn Estuary during the Holocene*. Unpublished MRes dissertation in Earth and Atmospheric Sciences, University of Reading.

Butler, S. (1988) Coastal change since 6000 BP and the presence of man at Kenn Moor, Avon. *Proceedings of the Somerset Archaeological and Natural History Society* 131, 1–11.

Canham, R. (1978) *2000 years of Brentford*. London, HMSO.

Caseldine, A. (1990) *Environmental Archaeology in Wales.* Lampeter, Department of Archaeology.

Caseldine, A. (2000) The vegetation history of the Goldcliff area. In M. G. Bell, A. Caseldine and H. Neumann *Prehistoric Intertidal Archaeology in the Welsh Severn Estuary.* York, Council for British Archaeology Research Report 120, 208–244.

Chambers, F. M., Mighall, T. M. and Keen, D. H. (1996) Early Holocene pollen and molluscan records from Enfield Lock, Middlesex, UK. *Proceedings of the Geologists Association* 107, 1–14.

Clapham, A. J. (2000) Waterlogged plant remains (Baker's Rithe and Russell's Lake), in M. J. Allen, and J. Gardiner (eds) *Our Changing Coast: a survey of the intertidal archaeology of Langstone Harbour, Hampshire.* York, Council for British Archaeology Research Report 124, 176–180.

Clayton, D. and Savory, H. N. (1990) The excavation of a Neolithic hut floor on Cefn Glas, Rhondda 1971–4. *Archaeologia Cambrensis* 139, 12–20.

Coles, J. M. (1978) The Somerset Levels: a concave landscape. In H. C. Bowen and P. J. Fowler (eds) *Early land allotment,* 147–148. Oxford, British Archaeological Reports British Series 48.

Coles, J. M. and Coles, B. (1998) Passages of time. *Archaeology in the Severn Estuary* 9, 3–16.

Coles, B. (2000) Somerset and the Street conundrum. In A. Harding (ed.) *Experiment and design.* Oxford, Oxbow Books, 163–9.

Coles, J. (1984) One swallow, one summer? A comment on a wooden stake in Kenn Moor. *Somerset Archaeology and Natural History* 128, 31.

Coles, J. (1989) Prehistoric settlement in the Somerset Levels. *Somerset Levels Papers* 14–32.

Coles, J. and Coles, B (1986) *Sweet Track to Glastonbury.* London, Thames and Hudson.

Coles, J. and Coles, B. (1998) Passages of Time. *Archaeology in the Severn Estuary* 9, 3–16.

Cooney, G. (2000) *Landscapes of Neolithic Ireland.* London, Routledge.

Cotton, J. and Green, A. (2005) Further prehistoric finds from Greater London. *London and Middlesex Archaeological Society* 55, 119–152.

Cowie, R. and Eastmond, D. (1997) An archaeological survey of the foreshore in the Borough of Richmond upon Thames. *London Archaeologist* 8, 87–93, 115–121.

Cressey, M. and Toolis, R. (1997) Solway Coastal Assessment. CFA Edinburgh University Unpublished Technical Report No.312. Commissioned by Historic Scotland.

Cressey, M., Dawson, A., Dawson, S., Milburn, P., Long, D. and Bunting, M. J. (1998) Solway Firth Coastal Assessment Survey Phase 2 1997. CFA Edinburgh University Unpublished Technical Report No. 384. Commissioned by Historic Scotland.

Cressey, M., Bunting, J., Dawson, A., Dawson, S., Long, D. and Milburn, P. (2001) Sea Level changes and Palaeoenvironment at Newbie Cottages, near Annan, Upper Solway Firth, South West Scotland. In B. Raftery and J. Hickey (eds) 2001 *Recent Developments in Wetland Research. WARP Monograph 2,* 257–270.

Cressey, M. (2001) Management options for the Newbie Cottages and Broom Knowes shoreline, Inner Solway Firth, south west Scotland. In E. Gordon and K. F. Leys (eds) *Earth Science And The Natural Heritage, Interactions and Integrated Management.* Chapter 12, 161–165. HMSO .

Crockett, A. D., Allen, M. J. and Scaife, R. G. (2002) A Neolithic trackway within peat deposits at Silvertown, London. *Proceedings of the Prehistoric Society* 68, 185–214.

Crone, B. A. (1998) *Dendrochronology of four timbers from the Solway Firth.* Unpublished report for Centre for Field Archaeology.

Cummings, V. (2000) Myth, memory and metaphor: the significance of place, space and the landscape in Mesolithic Pembrokeshire. In R. Young (ed.) *Mesolithic lifeways: Current Research from Britain and Ireland.* Leicester, Leicester Archaeology Monographs 7, 87–96.

Cunliffe, B. (2001) *Facing the Ocean.* Oxford University Press.

Dark, P. (forthcoming) Plant communities and human activity in the Lower Submerged Forest and Mesolithic occupation sites. In Bell, M forthcoming, *Prehistoric Coastal Communities: the archaeology of western Britain 6000–3000 Cal BC.* York CBA Research Report 149.

Darvill, T. (1982) *The Megalithic chambered tombs of the Cotswold-Severn Region*. Highworth, Vorda.

Darvill, T. (1984) Neolithic Gloucestershire. In A. Saville (ed.) 1984 *Archaeology in Gloucestershire*. Cheltenham: Cheltenham Art Gallery and Museums, 80–106.

Darvill, T. (1986) Neolithic Avon. In M. Aston and R. Iles (eds) *The Archaeology of Avon*. Bristol, Avon County Council, 13–28.

Darvill, T. (1987) *Prehistoric Gloucestershire*. Gloucester, Alan Sutton.

Dawson, S., Dawson A., Cressey, M., Bunting, J., Long, D. and Milburn, P. (1999) Newbie Cottages, Inner Solway Firth: Holocene relative sea level changes. In R. M. Tipping, (ed.), *The Quaternary of Dumfries and Galloway. Field Guide*, London, Quaternary Research Association, 98–104.

de Volder, A. (1998) *Sea level and vegetational changes at Redwick 1 on the Gwent Levels in the Severn Estuary*. Unpublished BA dissertation, Archaeology Department, University of Wales, Lampeter.

Devoy, R. J. N. (1979) Flandrian sea-level changes and vegetational history of the lower Thames estuary. *Philosophical Transactions of the Royal Society, London Series*, B285, 355–410.

Devoy, R. J. N. (1980) Post-glacial environmental change and man in the Thames estuary: A synopsis. In F. H. Thompson (ed.) *Archaeology and Coastal Change*, 134–148. Society of Antiquaries of London.

Dixon, P. (1994) *Crickley Hill I: The Hillfort Defences*. University of Nottingham.

Draper, J. C. (1958) Hampshire. Survey of islands in Langstone Harbour, *Hampshire Field Club and Archaeological Society Archaeological Newsletter* 6, 204.

Draper, J. C. (1961) Upper Palaeolithic type flints from Long Island, Langstone Harbour, Portsmouth, *Proceedings of the Hampshire Field Club and Archaeological Society* 22, 105–6.

Druce, D. (1998) Late Mesolithic and Early Neolithic environmental change in the central Somerset Levels: recent work at Burnham-on-Sea. *Archaeology in the Severn Estuary* 9, 17–30.

Druce, D. (2000) *Mesolithic to Romano-British archaeology and environmental change of the Severn Estuary, England*. Unpublished PhD thesis, Department of Archaeology, University of Bristol.

Drummond-Murray, J., Thomas, C. J. and Sidell, E. J. (1998) *The Big Dig. Archaeology and the Jubilee Line Extension*. London, Museum of London Archaeology Service.

Dyer, K. R. (1975) The buried channels of the 'Solent River', southern England. *Proceedings of the Geologists' Association* 86, 239–245.

Edmonds, M. (1999) *Ancestral Geographies of the Neolithic: Landscapes, monuments and memory*. London, Routledge.

Evans, J. G. (1972) *Land Snails in Archaeology*. London, Seminar Press.

Everard, C. E. (1954) Submerged gravel and peat in Southampton Water. *Proceedings of the Hampshire Field Club and Archaeological Society* 18, 263–285.

Ferris, I. and Dingwall, L. (1992) Archaeological investigations in 1992: the Gwent approaches to the Second Severn crossing. *Severn Estuary Levels Research Committee Annual Report 1992*, 39–44.

Field, D. (1989) Tranchet axes and Thames picks: Mesolithic core tools from the West London Thames. *Transactions of the London and Middlesex Archaeological Society* 40, 1–26.

Fulford M., Allen J. R. L. and Rippon S. J. (1994) The settlement and drainage of the Wentlooge Level, Gwent: excavation and survey at Rumney Great Wharf 1992. *Britannia* XXV, 175–211.

Gardiner, J. P. (1987) Tales of the unexpected: approaches to the assessment and interpretation of museum flint collections. In A. G. Brown and M. R. Edmunds (eds) *Lithic Analysis and Later British Prehistory*. Oxford, British Archaeological Reports British Series 162, 49–63.

Gardiner, J. P. (1988) *The Composition and Distribution of Neolithic Surface Flint Assemblages in Central-Southern England*, unpublished PhD thesis, Department of Archaeology, University of Reading.

Gardiner, J. P. (1996) Early farming communities in Hampshire. In D. A. Hinton and M. Hughes(eds) *Archaeology in Hampshire: a framework for the Future*. Hampshire County Council, 6–12.

Gardiner, J. P., Allen, M. J., Hamilton-Dyer, S., Laidlaw, M. and Scaife, R. G. (2002) Making the most of it: late prehistoric pastoralism in the Avon Levels, Severn Estuary. *Proceedings of the Prehistoric Society* 68, 1–39.

Gardiner, P. (2000) Excavations at Birdcombe, Somerset: Mesolithic settlement, subsistence and landscape use in the southwest of England. In R. Young (ed.) *Mesolithic lifeways: Current Research from Britain and Ireland* Leicester, Leicester Archaeology Monographs 7, 199–208.

Gates, T. (1975) *The middle Thames valley. An archaeological survey of the river gravels.* Oxford, Berkshire Archaeological Committee Publication no1.

Gibbard, P. L. (1985) *Pleistocene history of the Middle Thames Valley.* Cambridge University Press.

Gibbard, P. L. (1994) *Pleistocene history of the Lower Thames Valley.* Cambridge University Press.

Gibbard, P. L. (1999) The Thames valley, its tributary valleys and their former courses. In D. Q. Bowen (ed.) *A revised correlation of Quaternary deposits in the British Isles.* Bath, Geological Society special report 23, 45–58.

Gilbertson, D. D. and Hawkins, A. B. (1983) A prehistoric wooden stake and the alluvial stratigraphy of Kenn Moor, Avon. *Somerset Archaeology and Natural History Society* 127, 1–6.

Gilbertson, D. D., Hawkins, A. B., Mills, C. M., Harkness, D. D. and Hunt, C. O. (1990) The late Devensian and Holocene of industrial Severnside and the Vale of Gordano: stratigraphy, radiocarbon dating and palaeoecology. *Proceedings of the Ussher Society* 7, 279–84.

Gifford and Partners (no date) *A13 Thames gateway archaeological investigations.* Unpublished client report.

Girling, M. A. (1988) The bark beetle *Scolytus scolytus* (Fabricius) and the possible role of elm disease in the early Neolithic. In M. Jones (ed.) *Archaeology and the flora of the British Isles.* Oxford University Committee for Archaeology, 34–38.

Girling, M. A. and Grieg, J. R. A. (1985) A first fossil record for *Scolytus scolytus* (Fabricius) (elm bark beetle): its occurrence in elm decline deposits from London and the implication for the Neolithic elm decline. *Journal of Archaeological Science* 12, 347–351.

Godbold, S. and Turner, R. C. (1993) *Second Severn Crossing, archaeological response: phase 1 – the intertidal zone in Wales. Final Report.*

Godwin, H. (1945) A submerged peat bed in Portsmouth harbour. Data for the study of post-glacial history. IX. *New Phytologist* 44, 152–155.

Godwin, H. and Godwin, M. E. (1940) Submerged peat at Southampton, data for the study of post glacial history V. *New Phytologist* 39, 303–307.

Green, S. (1989) Some recent archaeological and faunal discoveries from the Severn Estuary Levels. *Bulletin of the Board of Celtic Studies* 36, 187–99.

Greig, J. R. A. (1982) Past and present lime woods of Europe. In M. Bell and S. Limbrey (eds) *Archaeological Aspects of Woodland Ecology.* Oxford, British Archaeological Reports International Series 146, 23–56.

Greig, J. R. A. (1989) From lime forest to heathland – five thousand years of change at West Heath Spa, Hampstead, as shown by the plant remains. In D. Collins and D. H. Lorimer (eds) *Excavations at the Mesolithic site on West Heath, Hampstead 1976–1981.* Oxford, British Archaeological Reports British Series 217, 89–99.

Greig, J. R. A. (1992) The deforestation of London. *Review of Palaeobotany and Palynology* 73, 71–86.

Haggart, B. A. (1995) A re-examination of some data relating to Holocene sea-level changes in the Thames estuary. In D. R. Bridgland, P. Allen and B. A. Haggart (eds) *The Quaternary of the lower Thames. Field guide.* Durham, Quaternary Research Association, 329–338.

Haggart, B. A. (1999) Pict's Knowe: Holocene relative sea level change. In R.M. Tipping (ed.) 1999. *The Quaternary of Dumfries and Galloway. Field Guide.* London, Quaternary Research Association, 62–74.

Haslett, S. K., Davies, P., Curr, R. H. F., Davies, C. F. C., Kennington, K., King, C. P. and Margetts, A. J. (1998) Evaluating late Holocene relative sea-level change in the Somerset Levels, southwest Britain. *The Holocene* 14, 115–130.

Haughey, F. (1999) The archaeology of the Thames: prehistory within a dynamic landscape. *London Archaeologist* 9 (1), 16–21.

Haughey, F. (2000) London's river: Working in a dynamic landscape. In L. Bonnamour (ed.) *Le fleuve gardien de la mémoire de la Saône: 150 ans de recherches archéoloques* 2, 108–113. Chalon-sur-Saône, Musée Denon.

Haughey, F. (2003) From prediction to prospection: finding prehistory on London's river. In A. Howard, M. Macklin and D Passmore (eds) *Alluvial Archaeology in Europe*. Lisse, Balkema, 61–68.

Haughey, F. (in press) Glimpsing the water. In *Proceedings of the 11th WARP International Conference on Wetland Archaeology, Edinburgh 2005*. Edinburgh, Society of Antiquaries of Scotland Monograph.

Haynes, F. N. and Coulson, M. G. (1982) The decline of *Spartina* in Langstone Harbour, Hampshire. *Proceedings of the Hampshire Field Club and Archaeological Society* 38, 5–18.

Heyworth, A. and Kidson, C. (1982) Sea-level changes in southwest England and Wales. *Proceedings of the Geologists Association* 93, 91–111.

Hillam, J. (1994) *The dating of oak timbers from the Wootton Quarr Survey, Isle of Wight*, Ancient Monuments Laboratory Report 47/91.

Hillam, J., Morgan, R. A. and Tyers, I. (1987) Sapwood estimates and the dating of short ring sequences. In R. G. Ward (ed.) *Applications of Tree-ring Studies, Current Research in Dendrochronology and Related Subjects*. Oxford, British Archaeological Reports International Series 333, 165–185.

Housley, R. A., Gamble, C. S., Street, M. and Pettitt, P. (1997) Radiocarbon evidence for the late-glacial human recolonisation of Northern Europe. *Proceedings of the Prehistoric Society* 63, 25–54.

Howard, A. J. and Macklin, M. G. (1999) A generic geomorphological approach to archaeological interpretation and prospection in British river valleys: a guide for archaeologists investigating Holocene landscapes. *Antiquity* 73, 527–541.

Hughes, G. (1996) *The Excavation of a late prehistoric and Romano-British settlement at Thornwell Farm, Chepstow, Gwent, 1992*. Oxford, British Archaeological Reports 244.

Hume, I. N. (1956) *Treasure in the Thames*. London, Frederick Muller Ltd.

Isle of Wight County Archaeological Unit (1999) *Isle of Wight Coastal Audit*, unpublished report prepared for English Heritage.

Jardine, W. G. (1863–64) Address of the President, December 1864 *Transactions of the Dumfriesshire and Galloway Natural History and Antiquarian Society, Series 1, Volume 2*.

Jardine, W. G. (1971) Form and age of late Quaternary shorelines and coastal deposits of southwest Scotland; critical data. *Quaternaria* 14, 103–14.

Jardine, W. G. (1975) Chronology of Holocene marine transgression and regression in southwestern Scotland, *Boreas* 4, 173–96.

Jardine, W. G. (1980a) Holocene raised coastal sediments and former shorelines of Dumfriesshire and Eastern Galloway. *Transactions of the Dumfriesshire and Galloway Natural History and Antiquarian Society* 55, 1–59.

Jardine, W. G. (1980b) (eds) *Glasgow Region, March–April 1980, Field Guide*. Glasgow, Quaternary Research Association.

Jarzembowski, E. A. and Jarzembowski, J. B. E. (1980) Two Thames foreshore deposits in West London. *London Naturalist* 59, 6–7.

Jennings, S., Orford, J. D., Canti, M., Devoy, R. J. N. and Straker, V. (1998) The role of relative sea-level rise and changing sediment supply on Holocene gravel barrier development: the example of Porlock, Somerset, UK. *The Holocene* 8 (2), 165–81.

Jones, H. (1988) Excavations at Bricklayers Arms Railway Depot site (Rolls Road, London SE1). Unpublished archive report, Museum of London.

Keith, A. (1911) Report on human and other remains from the Alexandra Dock extension,

Newport. In F. H. S. Knowles and A. Keith (eds) *Human and other remains found in the neighbourhood of Newport, Monmouthshire*. Newport Free Library and Museum Committee, 17–24.

Knowles, F. H. S. (1911) Report on human remains from the Ifton limestone quarries. In F. H. S. Knowles and A. Keith (eds) *Human and other remains found in the neighbourhood of Newport, Monmouthshire*. Newport Free Library and Museum Committee, 5–16.

Lawrence, G. F. (1929) Antiquities from the Middle Thames. *Archaeological Journal* 86, 69–96.

Levitan, B. M. and Smart, P. L. (1989) Charterhouse Warren Farm Swallet, Mendip, Somerset: Radiocarbon dating evidence. *Proceedings of the University of Bristol Spelaeological Society* 18, 390–4.

Lewis, J. S. C. (1991) Excavation of a late Glacial and early Flandrian site at Three Ways Wharf, Uxbridge: Interim report. In R. N. E. Barton, A. J. Roberts and D. A. Rowe (eds) *Late Glacial settlement in north-west Europe*. York, Council for British Archaeology Research Report 77, 246–255.

Lewis, J. S. C., Wiltshire, P. E. J. and Macphail, R. I. (1992) A late Devensian / Early Flandrian site at Three Ways Wharf, Uxbridge: environmental implications. In S. Needham and M. G. Macklin (eds) *Alluvial archaeology in Britain*. Oxford, Oxbow Monograph 27, 235–247.

Lewis, J. S. C. (2000) The Neolithic period. In MoLAS (ed.) *The archaeology of Greater London: an assessment of archaeological evidence for human presence in the area now covered by Greater London*. London, Museum of London Archaeology Service Monograph, 63–80.

Lewis, M. P. (1992) *The prehistory of coastal south-west Wales*. Unpublished PhD thesis, Department of Archaeology, University of Wales, Lampeter.

Lloyd, J. (1999) Priestside Flow: Holocene sea-level record and implications for sea-level change. In R. M. Tipping (ed.) *The Quaternary of Dumfries and Galloway Field Guide*. London, Quaternary Research Association, 87–97.

Locock, M. (2000) *Prehistoric settlement in southeast Wales: the lithic evidence* Unpublished report for Cadw. Swansea, Glamorgan-Gwent Archaeological Trust report no 2000/024.

Long, A. J. (1995) Sea-level and crustal movements in the Thames estuary, Essex and East Kent. In D. R. Bridgland, P. Allen and B. A. Haggart (eds) *The Quaternary of the Lower Thames. Field guide*. Durham, Quaternary Research Association, 99–105.

Long, A. J., Scaife, R. G. and Edwards, R. J. (2000) Stratigraphic architecture, relative sea-level and models of estuary development in southern England: New data from Southampton Water. In K. Pye and J. R. L. Allen (eds) *Coastal and estuary environments: sedimentology, geomorphology and geoarchaeology*. London, Geological Society Special Publication.

Louwe Kooijmans, L. P. (1993) Wetland exploitation and upland relations of prehistoric communities in the Netherlands. In J. P. Gardiner (ed.) *Flatlands and Wetlands: current themes in East Anglian archaeology*. East Anglian Archaeological Report 50, 71–116.

Lynch, F. (2000) The earlier Neolithic. In F. Lynch, S. Aldhouse-Green and J. L. Davies (eds) *Prehistoric Wales*. Stroud, Sutton, 42–78.

Lynch, F., Aldhouse-Green, S. and Davies J. L. (2000) *Prehistoric Wales*. Stroud, Sutton.

Macdonald, J. (1976) Neolithic. In D. Collins, J. Macdonald, J. Barrett, R. Canham, R. Merrifield and J. Hurst (eds) *The archaeology of the London area: Current knowledge and problems*. London, London and Middlesex Archaeology Society Special Paper no.1, 19–32.

Marsden, P. (no date) *A Roman ship from Blackfriars, London* London, Guildhall Museum Publication.

Masters, L. (1981) A Mesolithic hearth at Redkirk Point, Gretna, Annnandale and Eskdale District. *Transactions of the Dumfriesshire and Galloway Natural History and Antiquarian Society* 56, 111–14.

Maylan, N. (1991) Thornwell Farm. *Archaeology in Wales* 31, 22.

Meddens, F. M. (1996) Sites from the Thames Estuary wetlands, England, and their Bronze Age use. *Antiquity* 70, 325–334.

Mellars, P. and Dark, P. (1998) *Star Carr in context: new archaeological and palaeoecological investigations at the early Mesolithic site of Star Carr, North Yorkshire*. Cambridge, MacDonald Institute Monograph.

Merriman, N. (1987) A Prehistory for Central London? *London Archaeologist* 5(12), 318–326.

Merriman, N. (1992) Predicting the unexpected: prehistoric sites recently discovered under alluvium in Central London. In S. Needham and M. Macklin (eds) *Alluvial Archaeology in Britain* Oxford, Oxbow Monograph 27, 261–267.

Milne, G., Bates, M. and Webber, M. (1997) Problems, potential and partial solutions: an archaeological study of the tidal Thames, England. *World Archaeology* 29, 114– 129.

Milne, G., Battarbee, R., Straker, V. and Yule, B. (1983) The River Thames in London in the mid 1st century AD. *Transactions of the London and Middlesex Archaeological Society* 34, 19–30.

Milne, G. and Milne, C. (1982) *Medieval waterfront development at trig lane, London.* London, London and Middlesex Archaeological Society Special Paper no5.

Minnitt, S. (1982) Farmers and Field Monuments. In M. Aston and I. Burrow (eds) *The Archaeology of Somerset.* Bridgwater, Somerset County Council, 23–8.

Milburn, P. and Tipping, R. M. (1999) Cathrine Hill: Holocene vegetation history. In R. M. Tipping (ed.) *The Quaternary of Dumfries and Galloway. Field Guide.* Quaternary Research Association, 148–152.

Moffet, L., Robinson, M. A. and Straker, V. (1989) Cereals, fruits and nuts. In A. Milles, D. Williams and N. Gardner (eds) *The Beginnings of Agriculture.* Oxford, British Archaeological Reports International Series 496, 243–61.

MoLAS, (1998). *Thames foreshore adjacent to North End of New Globe Walk, London SE1.* Unpublished client report.

MoLAS (2000) *The archaeology of Greater London: an assessment of archaeological evidence for human presence in the area now covered by Greater London.* London, Museum of London Archaeology Service.

Mook, W. G. (1986) Business meeting: recommendations/resolutions adopted by the Twelfth International Radiocarbon Conference, *Radiocarbon* 28, 799

Mottershead, D. N. (1976) The Quaternary History of the Portsmouth region. *Portsmouth Geographical Essays* 2, 1–21.

Nayling, N. and Caseldine A. (1997) *Excavations at Caldicot, Gwent: Bronze Age palaeochannels in the Lower Nedern Valley.* York, Council for British Archaeology Research Report 108.

Norman, C. (1982) Mesolithic hunter-gatherers, 9000–4000 BC. In M. Aston and I. Burrow (eds) *The Archaeology of Somerset.* Bridgewater, Somerset County Council, 15–22.

Owen-John, H. (1988) The hillslope enclosure in Coed-y-Cymdda near Wenvoe, South Glamorgan. *Archaeologia Cambrensis* 137, 43–98.

Parkhouse, J. and Lawler, M. (1990) *Archaeology of the Second Severn Crossing* Gwent and Glamorgan Archaeological Trust.

Peglar, S. M., Fritz, S. C. and Birks, H. J. B. (1989) Vegetation and land-use history at Diss, Norfolk. *Journal of Ecology* 77, 203–222.

Perraton, C. (1953) The salt-marshes of the Hampshire-Sussex border, *Journal of Ecology* 41, 240–247.

Pitts, M. (2000) *Hengeworld.* London, Century.

Poole, H. F. (1929) Stone axes found in the Isle of Wight, Part 1. *Proceedings of the Isle of Wight Natural History and Archaeology Society* 1, 652–658.

Poole, H. F. (1936) An outline of the Mesolithic cultures of the Isle of Wight. *Proceedings of the Isle of Wight Natural History and Archaeology Society* 2, 551–581.

Preece, R. C. and Robinson, J. E. (1982) Mollusc, ostracod and plant remains from early postglacial deposits near Staines. *The London Naturalist* 61, 6–15.

Pryor, F. (1991) *Flag Fen Prehistoric Fenland Centre.* London, English Heritage.

Pryor, F. and Kinnes, I. (1982) A waterlogged causewayed enclosure in the Cambridgeshire Fens. *Antiquity* 56, 124–6.

Rackham, D. J. (1994) Prehistory in the Lower Thames floodplain. *London Archaeologist* 7 (7), 191–196.

Rackham, O. (1986) *The History of the Countryside.* London, Dent and Sons.

Raftery, B. (1996) *Trackway Excavations in the Mountdillon bogs, Co. Longford, 1985–1991. Irish Archaeological Wetland Unit Transactions: 3* Dublin, Crannog Publication.

Ramsey, C. B. (1995) Radiocarbon calibration and the analysis of stratigraphy: the OxCal program. *Radiocarbon* 37, 425–30.

RCAHMS (1997) *Eastern Dumfriesshire an archaeological landscape.* Edinburgh, The Stationary Office.

Reading, H. G. (1986) Facies. In H. G. Reading (ed.) *Sedimentary environments and facies.* Oxford, Blackwell Science, 4–19.

Reimer, P. J., Baillie, M. G. L., Bard, E., Bayliss, A., Beck, J. W., Bertrand, C., Blackwell, P. G., Buck, C. E., Burr, G., Cutler, K. B., Damon, P. E., Edwards, R. L., Fairbanks, R. G., Friedrich, M., Guilderson, T. P., Hughen, K. A., Kromer, B., McCormac, F. G., Manning, S., Bronk Ramsey, C., Reimer, R. W., Remmele, S., Southon, J. R., Stuiver, M., Talamo, S., Taylor, F. W., van der Plicht, J. and Weyhenmeyer, C. E. (2004) IntCal04 Terrestrial Radiocarbon Age Calibration, 0–26 cal kyr BP, *Radiocarbon* 46,1029–1058

Richards, M. P. and Hedges R. E. M. (1999) A Neolithic revolution? New evidence of diet in the British Neolithic. *Antiquity* 73, 891–7.

Robertson-Mackay, R. (1987) The Neolithic causewayed enclosure at Staines, Surrey: excavations 1961–63. *Proceedings of the Prehistoric Society* 53, 23–128.

Rogers, E. H. (1946) The raised beach, submerged forest and kitchen midden of Westward Ho! and the submerged stone row of Yelland. *Proceedings of the Devon Archaeological Exploration Society* 3, 109–35.

Saville, A. (1983) Excavations at Condicote Henge monument. Gloucestershire 1977. *Transactions of the Bristol and Gloucester Archaeological Society* 101, 39–45.

Saville, A. (1984) Palaeolithic and Mesolithic evidence from Gloucestershire. In Saville A. (ed.) *Archaeology in Gloucestershire.* Cheltenham, Cheltenham Art Gallery and Museums, 59–79.

Saville, A. (1990) *Hazelton North: The excavation of a Neolithic long cairn of the Cotswold-Severn group.* London, English Heritage Archaeological Report 13.

Savory, H. N. (1971) A Neolithic stone axe and wooden handle from Port Talbot. *Antiquaries Journal* 51, 296–7.

Savory, H. N. (1980) The Neolithic in Wales. In J. A. Taylor (ed.) *Culture and Environment in Prehistoric Wales.* Oxford, British Archaeological Report British Series 76, 207–231.

Scaife, R. G. (2000) Pollen analysis at Farlington Marshes: a vegetational history of Langstone Harbour. In M. J. Allen, and J. Gardiner (eds), *Our Changing Coast: a survey of the intertidal archaeology of Langstone Harbour, Hampshire.* York, Council for British Archaeology Research Report 124, 171–175.

Schulting, R. J. and Richards M. P. (2000) The use of stable isotopes in studies of subsistence and seasonality in the British Mesolithic. In R. Young (ed.) *Mesolithic lifeways: Current Research from Britain and Ireland.* Leicester, Leicester Archaeology Monographs 7, 55–66.

Seel, S. (2001) *Late prehistoric woodlands and wood use on the lower Thames floodplain.* Unpublished PhD thesis, University of London.

Serjeantson, D., Field, D., Penn, J. and Shipley, M. (1991) Excavations at Eden II, Kingston: environmental reconstruction and prehistoric finds. *Surrey Archaeological Collections* 81, 71–90.

Sidell, E. J., Scaife, R. G., Tucker, S. and Wilkinson, K. N. (1995) Palaeoenvironmental investigations at Bryan Road, Rotherhithe. *London Archaeologist* 7(11), 279–285.

Sidell, E. J., Scaife, R. G., Wilkinson, K. N., Giorgi, J. A., Goodburn, D., Gray-Rees, L. and Tyers, I. (1997) Spine Road Development, Erith, Bexley (RPS Clouston Site 2649): A Palaeoenvironmental Assessment. London, Museum of London Archaeology Service unpublished report.

Sidell, E. J., Wilkinson, K. N., Scaife, R. G. and Cameron, N. (2000) *The Holocene evolution of the London Thames.* London, Museum of London Archaeology Service Monograph 5.

Sidell, E. J., Cotton, J., Rayner, L. and Wheeler, L. (2002) *The prehistory and topography of Southwark and Lambeth.* London, Museum of London Archaeology Service Monograph 14.

Simmons, I. G. (1996) *The Environmental Impact of later Mesolithic cultures.* Edinburgh University Press.

Simmons, I. G. (2001) Ecology into landscape: some English moorlands in the later Mesolithic. *Landscapes* 21, 42–55.

Smith, A. G. and Pilcher, J. R. (1973) Radiocarbon dates and the vegetational history of the British Isles. *New Phytologist* 72, 903–914.

Smith, A. G. and Cloutman, E. W. (1988) Reconstruction of Holocene vegetation history in three dimensions at Waun-Fignen-Felen, an upland site in South Wales. *Philosophical Transactions of the Royal Society, London* B322, 159–219.

Smith, A. G. and Morgan, S. (1989) A succession to ombrotrophic bog in the Gwent Levels and its demise: a Welsh parallel to the peats of the Somerset Levels. *New Phytologist* 112, 145–67.

Smith, C. (1992a) *Late Stone Age hunters of the British Isles.* London, Routledge.

Smith, C. (1992b) The population of late Upper Palaeolithic and Mesolithic Britain. *Proceedings of the Prehistoric Society* 58, 41–76.

Smith, G. H. (1989) Evaluation work at the Druid Stoke megalithic monument, Stoke Bishop, Bristol 1983. *Transactions of the Bristol and Gloucestershire Archaeological Society* 107, 27–37.

Smith, R. (1984) The ecology of Neolithic farming systems as exemplified by the Avebury region of Wiltshire. *Proceedings of the Prehistoric Society* 50, 99–120.

Spurrell, F. C. J. (1889) On the estuary of the Thames and its alluvium. *Proceedings of the Geological Society* 11, 210–230.

Starkel, L. (1994) Reflection of the glacial-interglacial cycle in the evolution of the Vistula river basin, Poland. *Terra Nova* 6, 486–494.

Strachan, R., Ralston, I. and Finlayson, B. (1998) Neolithic and later prehistoric structures, and early medieval metal-working at Blairhall Burn, Amisfield, Dumfriesshire. *Proceedings of the Society of Antiquaries, Scotland* 128, 55–94.

Stuiver, M. and Becker, B. (1993) High-precision decadal calibration of the radiocarbon time-scale, AD 1950–6000 BC. *Radiocarbon* 33, 35–66.

Sykes, C. M. (1938) Some flint implements from Blackstone Rocks, Clevedon. *Proceedings of the University of Bristol Speleological Society* 15, 75–79.

Taylor, H. (1996) Time and Tide. A study of a site at Erith in the Thames Estuary. unpublished BA dissertation, Department of Archaeology, University of Sheffield.

Taylor, T. (2001) *Digging the dirt with Time Team.* London, Channel 4 Books.

Tebbens, L. A., Veldkamp, A., Westerhoff, W. and Kroonenberg, S. B. (1999) Fluvial incision and channel downcutting as a response to Late-glacial and Early Holocene climate change: the lower reach of the River Meuse (Maas), The Netherlands. *Journal of Quaternary Science* 14, 59–76.

Thomas, C. and Rackham, D. J. (1996) Bramcote Green, Bermondsey: a Bronze Age trackway and palaeoenvironmental sequence. *Proceedings of the Prehistoric Society* 61, 221–253.

Thomas, J. (1988) The social significance of Cotswold-Severn burial practice. *Man* 23, 540–559.

Thomas, J. (1991) *Rethinking the Neolithic.* Cambridge University Press.

Thomas, J. (1999) *Understanding the Neolithic.* London, Routledge.

Tilley, C. (1994) *A Phenomenology of Landscape: places, paths and monuments.* Oxford, Berg.

Tipping, R. M. (1997) The Environmental History of the Landscape, in *Eastern Dumfrieshire an archaeological landscape,* Edinburgh, The Stationary Office for the Royal Commission on Historic and Ancient Monuments of Scotland 10–23.

Tipping, R. M. (1999) Burnfoothill Moss: Regional vegetation and land-use change. In R. M. Tipping (ed.) *The Quaternary of Dumfries and Galloway Field Guide.* London, Quaternary Research Association, 117–122.

Tomalin, D. J., Loader, R. and Scaife, R. G. (forthcoming) *Coastal Archaeology in a dynamic environment: a Solent case study.* London, English Heritage Archaeological Report.

Tratman, E. K. (1967) The Priddy Circles, Mendip, Somerset. Henge Monuments. *Proceedings of the University of Bristol Spelaeological Society* 11 (1), 97–125.

Troels-Smith, J. (1955), Characterisation of unconsolidated sediments. *Danmarks. Geologiske Undersol IVR* 3 (101), 1–73.

Trump, B. (1962) The Origin and Development of British Middle Rapiers. *Proceedings of the Prehistoric Society* 28, 80–102.

Tyers, I. (1988) The prehistoric peat layers (Tilbury IV). In P. Hinton (ed.) *Excavations in Southwark 1973–76 and Lambeth 1973–79*. London, London and Middlesex Archaeological Society and Surrey Archaeological Society, 5–12.

Tyler, A. (1976) *Neolithic Flint axes from the Cotswold Hills*. Oxford, British Archaeological Reports British Series 25.

Van de Noort, R. (2004) *The Humber Wetlands: the archaeology of a Dynamic Landscape*. Macclesfield, Windgather Press Ltd.

Walker, M. J. C., Bell M. G., Caseldine A. E., Cameron N. G., Hunter K. L., James J. H., Johnson S. and Smith D. N. (1998) Palaeoecological investigations of middle and late Flandrian buried peats in the Caldicot Levels, Severn Estuary, Wales. *Proceedings of the Geological Association* 109, 51–78.

Walters B. (1992) *The Archaeology and History of ancient Dean and the Wye Valley*. Cheltenham, Thornhill Press.

Webber, M. (2004) The Chelsea club: a Neolithic wooden artefact from the River Thames in London. In J. Cotton and D. Field (eds) *Towards a New Stone Age*. York, Council for British Archaeology Research Report 137, 124–127.

Wells, J. B. (1999) Brighouse Bay: Coastal evolution and relative sea-level changes. In R. M. Tipping (ed.) *The Quaternary of Dumfries and Galloway. Field Guide*. London, Quaternary Research Association, 44–50.

Wheeler, R. E. M. (1929) 'Old England', Brentford. *Antiquity* 3, 20–32.

Whittle, A. (1993) The Neolithic of the Avebury area: sequence, environment, settlement and monuments. *Oxford Journal of Archaeology* 12, 29–53.

Whittle, A. (1997) Moving on and moving around, Neolithic settlement mobility. In P. Topping (ed.) *Neolithic Landscape*. Oxford, Oxbow Monograph 86.

Whittle, A. (1999) The Neolithic Period c. 4000–2500/2200 BC: changing the world. In J. Hunter and I. Ralston (eds) *The Archaeology of Britain*. London, Routledge, 58–76.

Whittle, A. and Wysocki M. (1998) Parc le Breos Cwm transepted long cairn, Gower, West Glamorgan: date, contents and context. *Proceedings of the Prehistoric Society* 64, 139–82.

Wilkinson, K. N. (1994) An examination of sediment from a sand eyot at Culling Road, Rotherhithe. Unpublished archive report, Cotswold Archaeological Trust.

Wilkinson, K. N. (1998) An investigation into the geoarchaeology of foreshore deposits at Bull Wharf. Unpublished archive report, Winchester, King Alfred's College, Winchester.

Wilkinson, K. N., Scaife, R. G. and Sidell, E. J. (2000) Environmental and sea level changes in London from 10,500 BP to the present: a case study from Silvertown. *Proceedings of the Geologists Association* 111, 41–54.

Wilkinson, K. N. and Bond, C. J. (in press) Interpreting archaeological site distribution in dynamic sedimentary environments. In T. C. Darvill and M. Gojda (eds) *One land, many landscapes*. British Archaeological Reports International Series, Oxford.

Wilkinson, T. J. and Murphy, P. (1988) *The Hullbridge Basin Survey: interim report no. 8*, Archaeology Section, Planning Department, Essex County Council.

Wilkinson, T. J. and Murphy, P. (1995) *The Archaeology of the Essex Coast, volume 1: the Hullbridge survey*. East Anglian Archaeology Report no. 71, Essex County Council.

Williams, J. (1970) Neolithic Axes in Dumfries and Galloway. *Transactions of the Dumfriesshire and Galloway Natural History and Antiquarian Society* 47, 111–122.